The

Emerging

HEALTHCARE

LEADER

LAURIE BAEDKE

NATALIE LAMBERTON

The
Emerging
HEALTHCARE
LEADER

A Field Guide

ACHE Management Series

Library of Congress Cataloging-in-Publication Data
Baedke, Laurie, author.
  The emerging healthcare leader : a field guide / Laurie Baedke and Natalie Lamberton.
    p. ; cm. — (ACHE management series)
  Includes bibliographical references.
  ISBN 978-1-56793-729-9 (alk. paper)
  I. Lamberton, Natalie, author. II. American College of Healthcare Executives, issuing body.
III. Title. IV. Series: Management series (Ann Arbor, Mich.)
  [DNLM: 1. Administrative Personnel. 2. Leadership. 3. Vocational Guidance. WA 525]
  R729.5.H4
  362.1068—dc23
                          2015000963

The paper used in this publication meets the minimum requirements of American National Standard for Information Sciences—Permanence of Paper for Printed Library Materials, ANSI Z39.48-1984. ∞ ™

Acquisitions editor: Tulie O'Connor; Manuscript editor: Jane Calayag; Project manager: Andrew Baumann; Cover designer: Marisa Jackson; Layout: PerfecType

Found an error or a typo? We want to know! Please e-mail it to hapbooks@ache.org and put "Book Error" in the subject line.

For photocopying and copyright information, please contact Copyright Clearance Center at www.copyright.com or (978) 750-8400.

Health Administration Press
A division of the Foundation of the American
    College of Healthcare Executives
One North Franklin Street, Suite 1700
Chicago, IL 60606-3529
(312) 424-2800

To my husband, Wes, and our beautiful children, Sophia and Quinn. This book could not have happened without your patience and encouragement. I love you.

To my mom, for instilling a passion for learning, and my dad, for modeling a tireless drive and pursuit of excellence. Thank you.

To those who have mentored me and shared so generously of their wisdom and experience, I am forever in your debt and pay it forward.

To Natalie, thank you for your partnership on this journey. You are an amazing woman and I am blessed to call you friend.

—Laurie

To my mom and dad, for teaching me to always do my best.

To my siblings, Nicole and Newman, for being my best friends.

To Laurie, for bringing me along on this wonderful adventure. I've learned so much.

Last but not least, to my husband, Rory, for his unwavering support of everything I am and everything I do. Thanks for being a shining example of an authentic leader and, most important, a lifelong partner.

Much love.

—Natalie

Contents

Foreword by Rulon F. Stacey, PhD, FACHE   xi

Introduction   xiii

Part I: Laying a Solid Foundation for a Successful You

Note to My 25-Year-Old Self
by Di Smalley, FACHE   3

1. Learn Self-Awareness   5
    What Is Self-Awareness?   6
    How to Gain Self-Awareness   11
    What Can Self-Awareness Do for You?   17
    Rookie Mistakes   20

2. Practice Self-Management   27
    How Self-Management Works   28
    Why Personality Matters   29
    When Weaving Work and Life Is Better Than
       Balancing Them   31
    What Would a Lifelong Learner Do?   34

Note to My 25-Year-Old Self
by Donald R. Avery, FACHE   41

3. Pay Attention to Your Character   45
    Integrity   48
    Honesty and Trustworthiness   52

	Accountability	54
	Credibility	55
	How to Strengthen Character	56
4.	Consciously Commit to and Exercise Self-Discipline	61
	Are You Up for Going All In?	62
	Why Mind the Little Things?	64
	What Should You Commit To?	67
	Strengthening Your Work Ethic	72
	Strategic Commitment, Not Sacrifice	73
	Rookie Mistakes	75

Part II: Building and Maintaining a Forward-Moving Career

5.	Cultivate Your Personal Brand	81
	Finding the True You	82
	Curating Your Online Posts	85
	Maintaining Professional Decorum	87
	Networking on Social Media	90
	Rookie Mistakes	92
6.	Identify and Develop Your Leadership Style	95
	Follow	96
	Learn from Mistakes	98
	Show You Care	99
	Pay Attention to Culture	100
	Take Ownership	102
	Be Cognizant of the Company You Keep	103
	Build on Your Inherent Strengths and Talents	106
	Note to My 25-Year-Old Self by William C. Schoenhard, LFACHE	111

7. Try, or Find Inspiration in, Servant Leadership 115
    The Benefits of Servant Leadership 117
    The Unassuming Acts of Servant Leaders 118
    Choosing to Be Brave, Not Popular 121
    Joining or Starting Difficult Conversations 123

8. Bounce Back from Failure 127
    Managing Failure 129
    Taking and Handling Criticism 131
    Persevering Through the Nos 133
    Trying New Things 137
    Forgetting 138
    Rookie Mistakes 139

9. Network, Network, Network! 143
    Networking Done Right 146
    Networking for Introverts 156
    Network Up 158
    Networking According to Your Season of Life 161

    Note to My 25-Year-Old Self
    by Deborah Y. Rasper, LFACHE 165

10. Engage a Mentor, Be a Mentor 167
    Identifying a Mentor 169
    Putting Together a Board of Career Advisors 171
    Getting Started 176
    Giving Back to the Field 178
    Rookie Mistakes 179

Part III: Opening Doors of Opportunity for Yourself

11. Grab That Internship! 185
    How It Works 187

Applying for an Internship   192
Create Your Own Internship   195
The End of Internship   197

12. Master the Job Interview   199
    The Preparation Stage   200
    The Interview Stage   206
    The Follow-Up Stage   211
    Salary and Benefits Negotiation   213

13. Own and Manage Your Career Path   217
    Don't Underestimate the Value of an
      Entry-Level Job   218
    Do Make It Happen   219
    Don't Get Comfortable   222
    Do Chart a Career Path   223
    Do Act *As If*   224
    Do Stand Out   226
    Do Make the Boss Look Good   227
    Do Win Employees Over, Especially Those
      Older Than You   229

Books That Teach, Advise, and Inspire Us   233
About the Authors   235

Foreword

HUNDREDS OF BOOKS are available to students and the business community. Many offer incredible insights into specific best practices of running an organization. Books on leadership, management styles, lean operations, and motivating and cultivating your workforce are readily available. There is also a subset of business books that dive into the particulars of the healthcare field. Books and speakers are plentiful for those who wish to learn how to navigate the ever-changing environment that is healthcare management. What has been lacking, until now, is a guide for students that bridges the gap between their academic pursuit and their first leadership role in healthcare.

More than theory, *The Emerging Healthcare Leader: A Field Guide* is your road map for that journey. A refreshing and practical tool, this should be your handbook, your back-pocket how-to resource as you traverse the early years of your leadership career.

In their engaging and authentic style, authors Laurie Baedke and Natalie Lamberton offer valuable insight, real-world examples, and sage wisdom that many do not accumulate until decades later in their careers. Additionally, what they so courageously share is the truth that successful people often fail. While Natalie and Laurie have achieved admirable successes, positions, opportunities, and accolades, they've also stumbled and misstepped along the way. Their willingness to share those experiences so that others can learn from them is a hallmark of great leadership. Each author has a proven track record of success in her short career.

I had the pleasure of meeting Natalie as my first fellow for the Poudre Valley Health System in Fort Collins, Colorado. She was an outstanding student and employee, and I could see her passion for healthcare way back then. She keeps good company, as through her I've had the opportunity to meet and get to know Laurie at the annual Congress of the American College of Healthcare Executives, where they've both served as faculty for the perennial favorite session "Developing the Next Generation of Leaders: Lessons from the First 10 Years."

This book is an undeniably compelling body of work, born from that successful Congress session. For good reason, students flock to that session to soak up the content, which has encouraged and equipped so many early careerists in healthcare administration over the years. Brimming with practical suggestions, lessons learned, stories, and anecdotes, the book offers wisdom from which newcomers to the field and industry veterans alike can learn.

Civil leader and philosopher Mahatma Gandhi once said, "The best way to find yourself is to lose yourself in the service of others." It has been a pleasure and a privilege to observe Natalie's and Laurie's journey. Their passion for investing in emerging leaders (those just a few short steps behind them), their commitment to excellence and personal development, and their tireless enthusiasm to serve and mentor gives me confidence that the next generation is in good hands. Healthcare needs great leaders—strong, humble, capable individuals who will rise to serve this profession. This book is a resource to equip them.

Rulon F. Stacey, PhD, FACHE
Chairman (2011–2012), American College of Healthcare Executives

Introduction

THIS BOOK—*The Emerging Healthcare Leader: A Field Guide*—is all about you. Not your parents, not your preceptors, not the seasoned CEO whom you aspire to become. We wrote it with your healthcare career in mind and with our industry knowledge and experiences as guides. Why? Our answer is threefold.

First, we believe in the enormous contributions you can impart. Today, you may still be learning or struggling to enter healthcare. But tomorrow, you will be among the principals in the field—whether making operational and workforce decisions for a patient care unit or an entire facility, consulting with chief executives and governing boards, running a physician or clinical practice, developing and implementing national policies and standards, or teaching future leaders. Before then, you need to seek out as much advice and insight as possible to mentally and emotionally prepare yourself for the changes and challenges (and the joys) ahead. And we wish to be part—even in a small way—of your journey to get there.

Second, we are passionate about healthcare. Working in this industry—regardless of your job title—is formidable but also an awesome, rewarding privilege. We want to see it become the best system in the world, and that can only happen if we put conscientious, well-trained, and caring people in the top positions. That starts with you. And you represent the next generation of leaders.

Third, we want to give back to the field. We are fortunate to have had countless mentors, colleagues, teachers, and superiors who graciously and generously invested time and effort in our own career development. This is why we have been so eager to return the favor by engaging graduate and undergraduate students year-round. We mentor them, review their resumés, and conduct mock interviews. Plus, we stay active and connected in the industry, an essential activity for any serious professional.

We designed the book to be a casual but an informative read—much like how we designed the early careerist sessions we present during ACHE's Congress on Healthcare Leadership. In fact, it was the positive reception to these sessions—along with the lessons we've both accumulated over the years—that convinced us to compile our advice and recommendations in book form. We can't be more thrilled to share these with you and a larger audience of emerging leaders.

WHO WE ARE

What makes us qualified to talk about career development? Like you, we were new to healthcare once, each armed only with a master's degree in health administration and a desire to be involved in something bigger than ourselves. Like you, we sought guidance from others and pursued multiple opportunities. Like you, we have worked extremely hard to get where we are today.

Laurie became a hospital vice president at age 22 and then went on to become a healthcare consultant, development coach, speaker, and brand strategist. Natalie—after a career as a schoolteacher and a college instructor as well as a stint as a director of a hospital's retail services—became a hospital CEO at age 29 and has since served in leadership positions for a number of healthcare organizations, coming full circle as a CEO again. We realize that our results are not typical, given that senior-level positions take years to attain. But our results are examples of what's possible when you commit yourself early to personal and professional development, to building relationships (which could one day lead to tremendous opportunities), and to presenting yourself as someone who is ready for the next level.

For six years now, we have presented a well-received early careerist session during Congress. This is a collaboration born out of our initial meeting seven years ago and our mutual interest in widening our professional scope and contributing to the field. Individually, we seize every opportunity to learn and to share that knowledge with up-and-comers—in or out of the industry.

Our education, ongoing training (Laurie is a Gallup-certified strengths performance coach), diverse experiences (Natalie was certified as an EMT), civic and professional activities, and everyday work duties give us a full picture of what a young careerist needs and wants.

WHAT THE BOOK IS AND IS NOT

This book is a guide, a reference, a resource, a companion manual. But it is *not* a textbook—nor is it your boss's or CEO's management book. It is yours—version 3.0. So put down your highlighter, grab your coffee mug, and get comfortable.

Superb graduate and undergraduate health administration programs do an excellent job at exposing their students to management and care-delivery scenarios in actual organizations. These programs even offer elective courses focused on professional decorum and skill development. And that's great!

Look at this book then as an extension of such a curriculum—and so much more. It is not stuffed with theories or academic language; instead, it is neatly packed with applicable strategies and straightforward (even amusing) examples. So if you want to know what self-awareness is, for example, the book does not go on and on about the philosophy and psychology of the self. Rather, it gives you practical tips on how to become self-aware.

The content is tailored to the particular concerns or curiosities of a new healthcare graduate trying to build or expand a career or even an established healthcare professional trying to switch disciplines, update or enhance existing skills, or learn ways to advise young protégés or students.

The 13 chapters here are divided into three parts. Part I (containing Chapters 1 through 4) discusses the art of self-awareness and self-management as well as the byproducts of these two concepts—strong character, conscious commitment, and self-discipline. These concepts are the foundation for the rest of the ideas in the book. Part II (containing Chapters 5 through 10) expands the Part I concepts and introduces more practices that you can adopt (or at least consider) now, including cultivating your personal brand, understanding your own leadership style, learning and rebounding from failures, creating lasting networking relationships, and mentoring. Part III (containing Chapters 11 through 13) covers the nitty-gritty of pursuing internship opportunities and being an intern, mastering the interview process, and managing your own career path.

Each chapter includes the following:

- An opening quote that represents the main essence of the chapter
- Reading Points, a list of the main topics in the chapter
- Remember These, a list of the lessons learned or takeaways from the chapter

Two more features, spread throughout the book, are worth mentioning:

- Rookie Mistakes, a sidebar of don'ts. We (and some of our colleagues) have made mistakes throughout our careers—lots of them. You can learn from these common mistakes now to avoid making the same ones in the future and to manage your response or reaction when (never if) you make mistakes.

- Note to My 25-Year-Old Self, a candid reflection by top healthcare executives. Each note is a mix of advice from the leader to himself or herself at a young age, general words of wisdom to early careerists, and reminiscences of past experiences and lessons. These leaders are so generous to share their thoughts (even their regrets and mistakes) with us, and we are very thankful.

At the end of the chapters, you will find Additional Resources and References, which we encourage you to check out for more information. At the end of the book, we offer our lists of books that were influential to our professional development and that remain our favorites.

One more thing: We understand the temptation to skim and skip chapters, but please don't! Here's why: We arranged the sequence of the chapters so that one lays out the foundation for the next, which in turn builds on the ideas of the previous one and sets up another layer for the next. It's an interlocking chain. If you jump ahead, you may miss a detail that links one concept or strategy to another and thus lose the full message. Read it over breakfast, on the commuter train to work or internship, or when you get tired of scrolling through your social media feed or playing addictive games on your phone. We don't care where you do it or how long it takes you. Just please read it from beginning to end.

CONCLUSION

We consider *The Emerging Healthcare Leader: A Field Guide* the beginning of our conversation with you, not the end. Please reach out to us. We can't wait to hear about your journey.

Laurie Baedke and Natalie Lamberton

PART I

Laying a Solid Foundation for a Successful You

No one has to tell you that healthcare management is complex; we're sure your professors, industry mentors, colleagues and bosses, textbooks and field literature, and personal or professional experiences have fully briefed you on that fact. The parade of challenges in a healthcare organization—including state and federal regulations, medical errors and other quality problems, accreditation mandates, revenue loss and cost-control issues, reimbursement cuts, technology obsolescence and advancements, workforce and patient demands, and physician pushback or dissatisfaction—is daunting. It's enough to make even seasoned managers and leaders scratch their heads.

No one has to tell you that this work—the work you have chosen to do—is mentally, physically, and emotionally draining. But it's fulfilling, too, and surprising (in a good way) and fun (in a thrilling, roller coaster kind of way).

No one has to tell you that the care delivery sector in which you're serving—including hospitals, medical centers, health systems, physician group practices, and other small and big facilities—is a large industry inside a huge industry inside the massive, high-stakes US healthcare system. It's like a "turducken" submerged in a pressure cooker.

No one has to tell you that the professionals who make up the healthcare delivery's workforce—from the primary care physicians and specialists to the nurses to the allied health practitioners to the administrators and senior leaders—are highly skilled, well educated and trained, credentialed, licensed, certified, and/or registered.

You know all this already. What you may not know is how you—the recent addition to the field—can stand out and start making your mark amid the constant swirl of changes and crises in your organization. This is where Part I of this book comes in.

Part I consists of chapters that discuss the fundamental principles, approaches, behaviors, and perspectives that you need to understand and then apply so that you can thrive in the healthcare workplace—or any workplace, for that matter. We stuffed these chapters with practical strategies, examples, mini-stories, recommendations, and glimpses into our own experiences. We did that to make the concepts as clear, relatable, and applicable as possible.

Remember this: The first decade of your career is your proving ground. Do as much as possible with that time and the opportunities that come your way, and do it while conducting yourself as well as you can. Part I shows you how to do that.

Note to My 25-Year-Old Self

When I was 25, I transitioned from being the head nurse for a med/surg unit and an ICU unit to being the director of professional relations for a different hospital in another state. That was all good, because one of the lessons I followed—and one I would give others—is don't ever take the same job twice. When my husband and I were being transferred, I was offered another head nurse position. I turned it down. It was a bigger hospital and a different patient population, but the job would not have given me the opportunity to learn anything new.

One of the things I wish I had known then was this: Know your strengths and weaknesses, and find positions that build on your strengths and minimize your weaknesses. At 25, I assumed I was (or at least could become) good at almost anything. I didn't appreciate what I have come to understand over the years: Everyone has natural talents. That doesn't mean you can't learn other skills, but there are certain abilities more ingrained in your personality than others. As an example, I excel at strategic thinking. That is a good thing in that it allows me to be a creative and innovative leader, but it is a bad thing in the face of financial restraints. Therefore, I know now that I must surround myself with folks who have their feet planted firmly in financial reality and can bring me back down to earth when needed.

Another thing I wish I had appreciated at age 25 was this: To be comfortable in your career, you must understand and accept your personal values and know the limits to which you will push them. When I was 25, I thought I needed to accept whatever my boss told me to do or to believe. As I have grown older, I now understand that not every boss in the world has a value system that is compatible with my personal values. When I look back on my

3

career, I realize that those times when I was most dissatisfied or uncomfortable with my work life had something to do with the variation between what I personally believed was right and what my boss or the organization I worked for believed. If your value system is not in sync with that of a potential employer, run—don't walk—away.

Finally, there is something I instinctively knew at 25 that I would tell any 25-year-old today. I am asked many times, "How did you get where you are today?" My answer is this: I volunteered for it. That doesn't mean I raised my hand and said, "Ok, I'll be the CEO!" What it means is that I have given every employer more than what they paid me for. If I see a job that needs to be done, I volunteer to do it—whether or not it is in my job description. Certainly, I believe that is one of the reasons I came to the attention of those in the position to hire me and advance my career. More important, volunteering has always given me a feeling of ownership and satisfaction in the organizations for which I have worked. It is part of the reason I can wake up every morning and say, "Thank God I get to go to work today." My prayer is that you can do the same.

Signed,
Di Smalley, FACHE
Chairman (2013–2014), American College of Healthcare Executives
Regional President, Mercy

CHAPTER 1

Learn Self-Awareness

"And you? When will you begin that long journey into yourself?"

—Rumi, 13th century Persian poet

Reading Points

- What Is Self-Awareness?

- How to Gain Self-Awareness

- What Can Self-Awareness Do for You?

PERSONAL—AND, BY EXTENSION, professional—development begins with an introspective self-evaluation. The more honest you are with yourself, the more eager you are to correct your faults or to accentuate your good qualities. This self-scrutiny is one of the hardest things to do for most people, yet it is the single most important path to self-awareness. A person who is self-aware, in turn, strives to be authentic, confident but humble, curious and open-minded, and eager to learn and improve. Wouldn't you like to work with or for a person like that? More important, wouldn't you like to be that kind of person?

This chapter discusses what all this means for someone like you—a recent entrant to the healthcare workforce. Here, we define self-awareness, offer common strategies for becoming self-aware, and list just a fraction of its many rewards. We also present examples from our own experiences.

WHAT IS SELF-AWARENESS?

The *Merriam-Webster Dictionary* defines the term as the "knowledge and awareness of your own personality and character." For the purpose of career growth, let's expand that meaning to include work strengths and weaknesses—related to skills and talents, interpersonal or communication styles, behaviors, habits, and so on. In other words, self-awareness refers to a person's understanding of his or her personal and professional traits, tendencies, behaviors, mind-set, abilities, and limitations.

Admittedly, getting to know yourself may feel unnatural. The self-reflection process is odd, frustrating, and even embarrassing; plus, the deliberate focus on you may make you feel like a narcissist (even without taking a selfie!). After all, it requires you to lower your defenses and raise your candor. If you've ever had a confrontation in which someone—typically, an authority figure—rattled off what's bad and good about you, then you already have an idea of the discomfort possible from this exercise. The good news is that you do this alone (for the most part), but the better news is that the results of your efforts are noticed and even applauded by those around you.

Being self-aware can yield many positives, including

- intimate knowledge of your character, strengths and weaknesses, and interpersonal style;
- better interactions and relationships, because you understand the need to improve the attitudes and behaviors you have that turn people off;

- greater influence on those around you, because your honesty, humility, and authenticity make you instantly relatable—even trustworthy;
- clearer vision of your career path, because you know what you can, cannot, and must do to advance your career; and
- stronger commitment to lifelong learning and growth, because you acknowledge you're a work in progress and need to continually improve.

All of these may position you for faster career advancement. Do note, though, that self-awareness alone is not enough to catapult you into the C-suite. Typically, you still need the education, knowledge, skills, and abilities to fill those roles and the years of experience and expertise to be truly effective. Self-awareness, however, is an essential foundation—no matter what your short-term and long-term goals are. Why? The more you know yourself, the better you can fix what's not working and boost what's working. It really is as simple as that.

Strengths and Weaknesses

The sooner in your career you recognize your strengths, the sooner you can enhance, share, and capitalize on them. And the sooner you acknowledge your weaknesses, the sooner you can improve them; work around them; or minimize their effects on others, your performance, or your reputation. Weaknesses aren't all bad, and they're not all major. But they always have the potential to trip you up or to diminish the value of your strengths.

Let's say a hospital's hiring manager is picking the new director of a patient advocacy office and is considering either Applicant A (master's degree, intern for an award-winning medical center, team player, comes off as cold and a know-it-all) or Applicant B (pursuing master's degree, fellow in a national association for patient advocates, organized and innovative, painfully shy). The manager would hire the applicant most likely to fulfill the job description and fit the organization's or department's culture. The manager is not going to explain to the one not picked why he or she didn't get the job, leaving the applicant bewildered about what went wrong with the interview, how the resumé could be revised, which qualification doesn't match, or what skill set or training is missing. But if the person is self-aware (read: knows his or her own strengths and weaknesses), the result may not be as mysterious; in fact, the self-aware applicant may have adjusted around the weaknesses before this point to ensure they do not upstage the strengths. (Back to the example: Who do you think got the job—Applicant A or Applicant B—and why?)

Although we are proponents of authenticity or letting your true self shine despite your flaws, we don't at all condone weaknesses that are or that lead to criminal, unethical, hostile, and harmful acts. Such a mind-set, feelings, and behaviors (e.g., racism, bigotry of any kind, extreme views, verbal and physical abusiveness, harassment of any kind, violent tendencies) have no place anywhere—especially not in healthcare, where people come to help and be helped. These negative traits must not be overlooked or viewed as personality quirks, and they must be addressed immediately.

The goal of identifying your strengths and weaknesses is *not* to transform you into a perfect specimen. (Newsflash: Nobody is perfect—regardless of how impressive and amazing an individual is; plus, self-aware individuals seek constant learning and improvement, not perfection.) The goal is to know and then to *act* on that information; it's like managing what can be measured, one of the quintessential leadership principles. After all, simply knowing is useless if nothing comes of it. Take us, for example; we both continue to take stock or self-evaluate, and we each do something about our respective discovery.

Natalie's strengths (or the "sweet spots," as we like to refer to them) are innovative thinking, big-picture and detail-oriented focus, persistence or tenacity, inclusive interaction with all the stakeholders in her organization, strategic planning, and crafting and implementing an organizational vision. Her weaknesses include having a cheerful personality, which those around her may find off-putting, especially when she's leading staff through tough challenges. In fact, a former board member once made this comment to her: "How are you going to be a leader? You're so small and so happy." Aware that this bubbly disposition could be viewed as an unbecoming trait for a leader, Natalie has worked on moderating the way she comes across. (See Chapter 2 for how she does it.) And she continues to work on this every day.

Laurie, on the other hand, finds her sweet spot to be as a catalyst and an architect of new businesses, initiatives, brands, or cultures. She is effective at designing, strategizing, executing, monitoring, and evaluating plans. She is a strong visionary, just like Natalie. Her weakness is impatience. Because she is task-oriented, she focuses on completing one step after another and occasionally forgets to pause (not intentionally) to align resources and gain support first for the new project. Now that she recognizes this tendency, she has made deliberate adjustments.

If you mitigate weaknesses and leverage strengths, you are in essence self-managing (the topic of Chapter 2). That is, you are taking action based on information you've gathered. More specifically, you are taking charge of your own circumstances and thus the opportunities that come your way. As such, you can move your career forward—in whatever industry and in whatever direction. And you can do all this efficiently and productively. Score!

Self-Management Example

For many people, the need for self-assessment or self-evaluation does not become obvious until they experience an event or a series of events (the "aha moment," the lightbulb turning on, the catalyst) that makes them wonder if they should make a change. This usually happens after a termination, a demotion, a bad performance review, dissatisfaction on the job, or a threat of being downsized. The following illustrates this type of scenario and the beginning of self-management (the act that follows self-awareness).

After graduating with a bachelor's degree in computer science, James landed a job with a healthcare software company. He was hired in the customer support department to help clients customize their software and troubleshoot their problems. He loved math and science in school and assumed that the logical thinking and problem solving required by the job fit his interests and degree well. (Plus, in a tight job market, he considered himself lucky for finding full-time employment period—let alone a job that had something to do with his major.) For two years, he struggled to enjoy or find satisfaction with work. He didn't like the repetitive nature of the job nor the rigid standards his department had to follow. He craved more, but he didn't know exactly what that meant.

When a position opened up in the development side of the company, James followed his gut and applied. He got the job! He was now responsible for designing certain software features and enhancements, and he was part of the team that developed programs from the ground up. For the first time, he felt like he was a contributor to the organization's vision and strategic goals, not just a cog in the wheel. His performance reviews showed his newfound happiness, and his clients and coworkers constantly complimented his ideas and work.

And that's when he started thinking about his career—specifically, moving up the organizational ladder; going back to school to obtain certifications, get more training, and update his skills; and joining a national association for healthcare information technology professionals to learn more about the industry. He also began to acknowledge that although he was good at logical thinking and problem solving, he was great at strategic and creative thinking (though he uses both sets of skills in his designs). Soon, he began winning awards and gaining a positive reputation.

Today, James looks back at those early years and is thankful for the experience. But he is convinced that if he took the time to do more self-reflection earlier (even before he graduated) and then began self-management—rather than just "hanging in there" and hoping for things to improve—he could have advanced in the company much sooner.

HOW TO GAIN SELF-AWARENESS

There's more than one way to become self-aware. For example, Anthony K. Tjan (2012), founder of a venture capital firm and a blogger for the *Harvard Business Review*, proposes a three-pronged approach: (1) testing and knowing yourself, (2) watching yourself and learning in the process, and (3) understanding others' self-awareness. Plus, many hospitals, health systems, health administration programs at colleges and universities, medical schools, healthcare professional associations, healthcare consultants, physician and executive coaches, and other groups offer seminars and webinars, academic courses, continuing education training, publications (e.g., books, articles, white papers, studies), and other resources on recognizing, honing, and applying self-awareness. Also available are the plethora of personality tests and 360-degree assessments you can self-administer or pay someone to run for you. Some of these tests are general, but some are healthcare specific. (Examples are Myers-Briggs, Kiersey Temperament Sorter, StrengthsFinder, DiSC, and Predictive Index.)

Our recommendations for gaining self-awareness—or embarking on that journey, because you could spend a lifetime discovering yourself or new things about you—are rooted in the same principles as those discussed in the existing literature or taught in educational programs. But ours are less formal and start at the ground level—where you are now, instead of where you want to be in the future. These are things you can do today.

Embrace Humility

A trademark of the most self-aware people is humility. Modest people—those who don't brag about their own talents and accomplishments but are quick to congratulate or compliment others on theirs—are inspirational. They do everything with integrity and are focused on serving others. They understand (and are even apologetic for) their weaknesses, and constantly invite others to help them improve and grow. They consider their strengths as gifts of luck and opportunities and as products of other people's hard work and generosity. They have a lot to teach (and they do often), but they insist they are merely students. They are confident in their abilities, but they admit not to know everything. They treat everyone with respect and recognize their value—regardless of what those people can do, contribute, or help with; they don't use people to advance their own agenda.

Being humble draws people in and thus expands one's sphere of influence. But we admit true humility (not false modesty) takes a lot of discipline and years to cultivate. It may not be easy for young careerists to balance the professional need to make their mark (e.g., showing what you can do, proving your proficiency or expertise, expecting and wanting credit for your contributions, getting seen and heard to land opportunities) with the personal desire to be modest—at least not when they just got a job. Having said that, it is possible to be a humble young professional (and there are many such careerists out there). It starts with getting real with yourself.

Commit to Getting Real with Yourself

Just as you need to take basic math before you can take advanced math, you need to adopt basic honesty before you can move on to self-awareness. Without basic honesty, you may find it impossible (not just difficult) to admit that you have flaws and limitations, that you need to step outside yourself to gain perspective, that you need help, that you don't know nearly as much as you believe, and that you need to make adjustments.

You can't be honest if you're not humble or if you're too proud. Your pride—which may stem from your achievements, high self-esteem or sense of worth, or upbringing—can block you from seeing the truth. For example, if at a young age you won a prestigious, merit-based award (this also applies to scholarship, publication, first-place win in a competition, or any coveted selection by a distinguished jury), you may see that as proof that you have reached the level of the best and as unwritten permission to feel self-satisfied. By all means, be proud of what you've achieved, but have some perspective, too. What an award gives its recipients is a start—a chance to do more with their skills, talents, and potential. It shouldn't be used as a pass to boast endlessly, which alienates people in the process. Don't ever think you can learn little else going forward.

Moderate your pride by seeking feedback from those who know you and those who can be completely honest with you. Feedback is the surest way to show you the attitudes, perspectives, traits, and behaviors you display but you don't get to observe yourself. When you receive the feedback, try not to be defensive because that would only hinder the process. Instead, take notes and ask for clarification if needed. Carefully think about the comments, especially the negative ones because those are the toughest to deliver but are the most enlightening. Then, decide how you will act on the information you have.

Doing nothing is a complete waste of everyone's time and effort. But doing something half-heartedly is worse, because you may give up the first time you encounter a slight difficulty and then go back to step one. Taming your pride requires you to go all in, to "man up" and take the pain and discomfort associated with honest self-reflection or getting real with yourself.

Develop a Habit of Self-Evaluation

Your behavior, attitude, perspective, motivation, wants, needs, priorities, and preferences evolve as you experience life and career changes. For example, as an unmarried, child-free, just graduated individual, your focus is likely on landing a decent-paying full-time job in your field of interest. As you learn more skills and gain greater proficiency, your focus may shift to career advancement—a promotion, a lateral move, a job transfer, more training, or a return to school. As your life and career progress to include more obligations and responsibilities (like a growing family, a mortgage, or a demanding position that requires community leadership), your focus will shift again. Through all these seasons or stages of life, your strengths and weaknesses and your general mind-set change, too. So it's important for you to do a regular self-evaluation (e.g., quarterly, annually, after a big project) to ensure that what you know about yourself (self-awareness) is keeping pace with how you've evolved as a person and as a professional.

Regular self-assessment doesn't have to be complicated; the old-school system of jotting down lists with pen and paper works well. Review the list immediately (don't procrastinate). Add notes on how you plan to improve, address, or discuss the items that need the most attention. You may set a date of completion for the specific items, or you may leave them open-ended. Whatever you do, make sure you keep this list in mind as you go about your days. Revisit it often, tape it to your desk, enter it into your smartphone, write about it in a private blog or diary, and update it if needed. Again, whatever you do, don't forget it—especially when you get busy.

Here are some questions to guide you while you do a self-assessment—quarterly, annually, or even after a big project:

- Whom do you communicate best with—in your personal life and at work? Why?
- What parts of the job come easiest to you? Hardest?

- What pitfalls seem to sink you every time? What bumps or barriers do you have to leap over? Why? How can you avoid them?
- How do you feel when you complete a task or project—especially the challenging ones?
- How do your family members, friends, work colleagues, superiors, and others (e.g., CEO, other senior leaders, volunteers, support staff, clinicians, vendors) perceive or describe you? What do you think they say about you behind your back?
- What parts of your job are most gratifying or rewarding?
- What tasks or projects do you tend to dread, avoid, or procrastinate on?
- Do you ask others for feedback after you complete a project or in general?
- Do you think you are making a difference? For whom? For what? How?
- Where in the organization or your personal life are you making the greatest impact?
- Are you growing in your position? If not, why?

Also, think about a recent mistake or failure. Dissect the circumstances to examine how you can learn from that event.

Regular self-reflection is important, not just for early careerists but also for every professional regardless of industry or job title. People who don't reflect are less self-aware and thus tend to have an interpersonal style that alienates, belittles, and lowers morale of others.

Nurture Your Curiosity

Albert Einstein has said, "The important thing is not to stop questioning. Curiosity has its own reason for existing." For our purposes, the reason may be that the US healthcare system needs curious leaders because curious people are fundamentally brave. They are not afraid to pose 101 questions—even the stupid and already answered ones. They are not intimidated to try new things, meet new people, or even retry old things with old people. They don't blink or break a sweat in the face of progress, changes, and challenges. Plus, curious people have a scientific mind; they approach everything with the scientific method—consider a question or problem, research that question fully, form a hypothesis, test that hypothesis several times, analyze the results of those tests, build a conclusion, and tell everyone about it so that actions can be taken.

Curiosity is a natural impetus for self-awareness. That is, if you are curious, you are eager to find out what and who makes you tick—and then you can leverage that discovery to grow personally and professionally and improve performance. And you do all this in a rigorous manner, as a scientist does. You might discover that curiosity is one of your strengths, and that's an excellent finding because it means you can perpetuate the learning that brings about and accelerates growth. Plus, the more you learn, the more curious you get.

So how can you nurture that curiosity, that insatiable spirit in you? Ask questions, and contemplate the answers. Communicate (either verbally or in writing) with people who interest you and who have unique experiences and opinions. Ask for advice and follow it (it doesn't matter if it works; what matters is that you were open to trying it). Read as much as possible; attend lectures or seminars; keep a journal; do a Web search and follow relevant links (you'll end up in a much different place than where you started); and join discussions—but listen so much more than talk (this is different from not having confidence, as discussed later).

We are all curious in varying degrees and typically about something or someone outside of ourselves. As proof, just look around you. If you turn up that curiosity and turn it inward, just imagine the kinds of conclusions you could draw about yourself.

WHAT CAN SELF-AWARENESS DO FOR YOU?

As we mentioned, self-awareness offers numerous advantages. Here are just a few of the many.

Authenticity and Trust

One of the most important benefits of self-awareness is finding the authentic, multidimensional you—the good, the bad, and the ugly of your character. Your authenticity lowers people's defense mechanisms because it tells them, "I'm a work in progress, and I'm trying my best." This encourages people to level with you, to be kinder, and to accept the qualities that make you different from them and those that make you just like them.

When you are authentic,

- you don't have a split personality—you speak and act the same way in public (in front of mixed company) as you do in private (in front of only those you trust);
- you make mistakes and poor decisions, but you acknowledge and apologize when you are wrong and you don't blame everyone else;
- you are honest with yourself and those around you, even if your honesty could put you in an unflattering light;
- you can admit "I don't know" and "I need help" without shame;
- you are not afraid to show sadness, anger (i.e., irritation and exasperation, **not** temper tantrums, abusive conduct, or blind rage), disappointment, fear, confusion, or doubt—emotions that may be perceived as weak;
- you show real concern for and desire to help with people's predicaments; and

- you "practice what you preach," and you do so according to your own belief system—not according to popular opinion or trendy practice.

This kind of behavior enables you to connect with others and earn their trust.

Stephen M. R. Covey (2008)—son of the late management expert Stephen R. Covey, who authored the popular *7 Habits of Highly Effective People*—wrote about instant trust in his book, *The Speed of Trust*. (Instant trust is a relatively new idea that is in contrast to the old—but still valid—model of earning trust only after a long time of proving yourself.) The book summarized Covey's thesis about trust in the subtitle: "the one thing that changes everything." How so? Trust is a currency, and if you have it you can do just about anything. But if you are self-aware, you will likely use that currency for good and be very transparent with what you do with it.

Influence and Style

Healthcare administration is a stressful 24/7 job, so you need to surround yourself with people whose support you can count on. Your interpersonal style—whether you're introverted, charismatic, strategic, creative, compassionate, driven, laid back, or something else in between—plays a big role (next to the strength of your character—such as your integrity, accountability, and credibility) in expanding or diminishing your influence over others.

This isn't about being liked or being popular, because at the end of the day a CEO or any leader is not worried about who likes him or her. (Generally, when you're kind, you don't have to wonder if people like you. The reverse is also true.) This is about understanding your own style's effect on others and making adjustments to your approach so that you can forge connections and relationships with those whom you can help and who will, in turn, help you get things done.

Every interaction you have is an opportunity for people to judge you (your personality and character) and an opportunity for you to evaluate whether you're conveying your strengths or highlighting your weaknesses. If the former, your influence may grow; if the latter, your influence may suffer.

You may ask yourself the following questions when evaluating your style and thus your influence. (Always elaborate on your answers to better explore your thinking or rationale.)

- Am I able to connect with leaders—both the formal and the informal? How?
- Am I able to engage colleagues, staff, boss, executives, patients, clinicians, and other stakeholders? How?
- Am I drawn to people or processes? Why?
- Am I more comfortable with one-on-one or group interaction? Why?
- Do I tend to say "let's do it" or "you do it"?
- How would I and others characterize my style? Am I comfortable with that?
- Do I prefer to deal with the big picture or the details?
- Is planning or implementation my sweet spot?

Confidence

As you become more self-aware, your confidence rises and your anxiety lessens. The confidence comes from knowing your strengths and weaknesses. When you reach this level of self-awareness, you will no longer be content to sit (and doodle—yep, we know what you're doing) in meetings, half-heartedly listening to the bigwigs discuss the issues and nervously waiting for your turn to report on your project (if you get that turn). You will speak up when appropriate, politely but decisively. Beyond meetings, you will get involved in the daily life of the department, unit, or office. You will contribute, according to your knowledge and capabilities. You will start acting like a self-aware leader, building relationships, giving compliments and credits to deserving individuals and groups, learning about everything, gaining trust, and managing your career.

One last note: Do not confuse confidence with boastfulness. Boastful people are typically insecure. Their desire to be noticed and praised is endless, and they get their validation from people's reaction (especially envy) to their accomplishments. Confident people, on the other hand, are typically secure. They are fully aware of who they are, what they have, what they know, and what they can do. Although they are proud of their accomplishments (and will boast about them only to thank and applaud people who have helped or maybe even to trash-talk as a joke), they don't gloat or show off. They understand that the true reward or payoff comes not from fleeting or even insincere praises but from the tangible outcomes.

Rookie Mistakes

Getting Caught in the Comparison Trap

Be honest, when was the last time you chided yourself for not having someone else's body or brains or talent or relationship or family? How about their car or house or income? How about their job title, education, social status, or accomplishments?

It's tempting and even natural to compare yourself to others. We all do it in one way or another. For example, when Laurie first joined the entrepreneurial (read: independent contracting) world of healthcare consulting, she occasionally thought those with traditional jobs had it better. They received a predictable paycheck every month or every other week, and they didn't have to worry about where their next project would come from. Likewise, other career rookies may long for the

→

salary and benefits their contemporaries earn, may disparage others' professional wins because of jealousy or rivalry, or may become downright depressed and resentful about the opportunities that stubbornly evade their path but that seem to flow straight into others' path. Simply, comparisons may be common, but they can trap you in an unproductive, exhausting cycle of coveting, envy, and self-loathing.

You could break this cycle by focusing on what you have; what you have contributed; and what you have achieved using your own wit, skills, and courage. Then, figure out what you need to do to be happy with the choices you made. That's exactly what Laurie did. She sat back, accepted that "it's not greener on the other side," and took an inventory of her life and career. She realized her job allowed her time, space, and flexibility that those traditionally employed lacked. She could build lasting and rewarding relationships, engage in a variety of challenging work, pursue leadership opportunities in professional associations, and entertain limitless opportunities—both in and out of work.

Pretending To Be Someone You're Not

An extreme consequence of comparing yourself to others is subconsciously or consciously absorbing their most desired qualities into your own persona. For example, if you admire your Facebook friend's volunteer activities, you might add that information on your resumé or mention it to an interviewer even if you haven't volunteered anywhere before. The same goes for work experiences, schools attended, hobbies, social and political affiliations, honors received, papers published, and even personal philosophies. You might think that doing so is harmless, the detail will impress other people,

→

and your "little white lie" will not get discovered. But you are wrong, and here's why.

First, you are committing a form of identity theft (at worst) and an unequivocal, untenable lie (at the least). Second, the good impression you may leave on a job screener is fleeting when compared with the long-lasting bad impression you will leave on everyone else. Third, hiring managers and human resources staff make phone calls to check the details on a resumé and the claims you make during an interview; at the very least, they will Google. Fourth, even if you get away with this unseemly tactic, the job (or the people you lied to) will eventually force you to apply what you claim to know or have done. And if you can't back up your words with action, you can't expect to remain in that position.

So skip all that drama! Be authentic. Own who you are, and don't you dare apologize for it. Remember that the online and offline personae most people display in public are the edited versions and not the rough drafts. In reality, their lives are less impressive. Fibbing only causes you stress and confusion about your career direction.

Being a Watcher, Not a Doer

When you're just starting your career, it's sometimes easiest to go along with the crowd and adopt the herd mentality. You're sitting in a meeting, and everyone agrees with the boss that option A is the best resolution for problem B. You nod your head and smile along with the group, even if your instinct tells you there's a better solution.

That's understandable. The healthcare workplace is very intimidating. All the decisions made there are either life or

→

death or affect a large cluster of people. Everything is a process with multiple steps. People walk and talk fast, and you're expected to keep up. Early on, almost everyone is older and more experienced than you. Thus, your natural response is to anxiously listen and observe, not participate.

Don't do that. You were hired for a reason, so show everyone what you can do. Listen intently, but join the conversation as well. State your opinions and back them up with evidence, which means you have to do your homework and prepare as much as possible. Volunteer for projects that will showcase your skills, but also be willing to take risks and challenges. Jump on as many opportunities as possible to learn and contribute with gusto. Your enthusiasm, eagerness, and confidence will be duly noted.

Investing Too Much in Your Weaknesses, Not Enough in Your Strengths

Don't get us wrong: We recommend improvement in all areas, and minimizing or eliminating weaknesses is a beneficial exercise. What we're saying is you should not pour all of your precious resources—time, money, physical and mental energy, and patience—into correcting a personality or professional deficiency while ignoring your promising qualities and innate talents. Strengths need as much (or even more) attention as weaknesses, depending on the position you hold.

Let's say you are terrible at small talks but excellent at public or group speaking. Determine which skill is more useful to the job you have today and the job you want in the near future. Then, devote an appropriate amount of resources to developing each skill. Ask yourself what you'll get out of each investment. For example, would learning how to chat improve your interactions, would it make your daily duties easier, and

→

would it increase the chances of landing your dream job? Likewise, would refining your public speaking make you more persuasive and informative, boost your department's/organization's reputation internally and in the community, get you a raise or promotion, or give you a competitive edge?

Here's a fun visual: Weigh the resources you put in against the results you get out. If the resources are much heavier than the results, then you can lighten the resources load significantly. You don't want this scale to balance, you want the results to be heavier (even a bit) than the resources. More bang for your buck!

Unfortunately, many new careerists (including us when we were starting out) favor fixing weaknesses over enhancing strengths. And many human resources departments and supervisors do as well. But we all need to change that mindset so that we're not wasting our resources on things that may not pay off in the long run.

Remember These

- Self-awareness refers to a person's understanding of his or her personal and professional traits, tendencies, abilities, and limitations.
- A person who is self-aware strives to be authentic, confident but humble, curious and open-minded, and eager to learn and improve.
- If you mitigate weaknesses and leverage strengths, you are in essence self-managing or taking charge of your own circumstances and thus the opportunities that come your way.

→

- Do a regular self-assessment to ensure your self-awareness is keeping pace with your personal and professional evolution.

- Regular self-reflection is important not just for early careerists but also for every professional, regardless of industry or job title. People who don't reflect are less self-aware and thus tend to have an interpersonal style that alienates, belittles, and lowers morale of others.

- The trademark of the most self-aware people is humility.

- You can't be honest if you're not humble or if you're too proud. Your pride can block you from seeing the truth.

- Curiosity is a natural impetus for self-awareness. That is, if you are curious, you are eager to find out what makes you tick—and then you can leverage that discovery to grow personally and professionally and improve performance.

- One of the most important benefits of self-awareness is finding the authentic, multidimensional you—the good, the bad, and the ugly. Your authenticity lowers people's defense mechanism, which leads them to connect with and trust you.

- As you become more self-aware, your confidence rises and your anxiety lessens.

- Do not confuse confidence with boastfulness. Boastful people are typically insecure, while confident people are typically secure.

REFERENCES

Covey, S. M. R. 2008. *The Speed of Trust: The One Thing That Changes Everything.* New York: Free Press.

Tjan, A. K. 2012. "How Leaders Become Self-Aware." *Harvard Business Review* Blog Network. Posted July 19. http://blogs.hbr.org/2012/07/how-leaders-become-self-aware/.

ADDITIONAL RESOURCES

Green Peak Partners. 2014. "When It Comes to Business Leadership, Nice Guys Finish First." http://greenpeakpartners.com/resources/pdf/6%208%2010%20 Executive%20study%20GP%20commentary%20article_Final.pdf.

Tobak, S. 2013. "Seven Signs You Are Not as Self-Aware as You Think." www.inc .com/steve-tobak/7-signs-youre-not-as-self-aware-as-you-think.html.

CHAPTER 2

Practice Self-Management

"We cannot change what we are not aware of, and once we are aware, we cannot help but change."

—Sheryl Sandberg, COO, Facebook

Reading Points

- How Self-Management Works

- Why Personality Matters

- When Weaving Work and Life Is Better Than Balancing Them

- What Would a Lifelong Learner Do?

NOW THAT YOU'VE done some self-reflection and have gotten acquainted with your strengths and weaknesses, you may wonder, "What's next?" Self-management—that's what.

Essentially, self-management is about being accountable for your own actions—in general or for a specific purpose—while relying on your own strengths and resources. When you manage yourself, you are policing your own behavior and adjusting it to attain a desired outcome. This requires not only self-awareness but also mental toughness and discipline, because self-management could lead you through ugly and awkward choices and eventually to change.

Ever been on a strict diet? Ever had to live on a small budget? Ever had to position yourself for a raise or a promotion? A "yes" to any of these questions means a "yes" to having done a form of self-management before. This chapter discusses how self-management works and what personal and professional areas in your life can be enhanced by it.

HOW SELF-MANAGEMENT WORKS

Self-management is mind-bogglingly useful. It is applied by many individuals, groups, and industries to many types of goals and objectives. Want to reduce stress, save money for retirement, monitor an illness, meet and mingle with the right people? Then self-management is just the thing for you! We know this sounds like a too-good-to-be-true course taught in your local community center, but the process is legit (that is, legitimately helpful and legitimately awesome).

The components common in self-management include these:

1. Identifying the problem to be solved, the goal to be accomplished, or the task to be performed (What do I want to do?)
2. Selecting the method, timeline, and/or strategies to be followed (How do I want to do it, and when?)
3. Monitoring your progress along the way, and making adjustments or corrections as necessary (How am I doing?)
4. Analyzing the outcome (How did I do? What did I learn?)

Of course, the components change according to who's doing the self-management and what purpose and industry it's for. And, of course, no one is required to follow these components (after all, they're not steps), but some use them as a guideline to organize their self-management effort.

What these components clearly convey is that self-management involves choices, and those choices are influenced by self-awareness. For example, if you've discovered that aversion to change is a weakness, you could opt to improve it or live with it. If you pick improvement, you are faced with myriad strategies for accepting and dealing with change. If you choose to live with it, you must consider the various consequences that will follow. Among these consequences is the possibility that you will experience slower career growth than your peers despite your superior strengths. As we mentioned in Chapter 1, some weaknesses eclipse strengths; aversion to change is an unfortunate weakness to have in an industry that is famous for its constant changes.

Now a warning: Practicing self-management doesn't automatically lead to great outcome. You could set goals, choose the best strategies, and check your progress periodically all you want. But if you're not doing the work necessary to change or adjust the behavior, none of your results will show any improvement.

WHY PERSONALITY MATTERS

Your personality—a character trait that makes you *you*—is part of the many factors that makes people want to engage with or disengage from you. That personality comes across in your interactions—whether on a personal or professional basis. So managing your interpersonal style and how you are perceived is important. (See Chapter 3 for a complete discussion of character.)

By "managing," we don't mean that you should pretend to be someone other than your true self or conceal (but not reverse) your bad qualities. We mean you should continually assess the impression you leave (good or bad) after an interaction and then amend the behavior that diminishes your message and intention. Take us, for example.

For Natalie, self-management is all about paying attention to people's reaction to her. She asks for and accepts feedback and adds that to the information she gathers on her own so that she can process all of it internally. She's aware of her bubbly, perky, or exuberant disposition, an inner joy that shows on her face; she's always smiling. On the surface, this is awesome because she is approachable. Plus, imagine a CEO who is upbeat even at the crack of dawn! But there's a *but* here. It isn't everyone's cup of tea. More important, it undermines her professional edge, not to mention the gravity of her position. It may lead those who don't know her to dismiss her as someone who is just silly and thus not to be taken seriously, but that's the farthest from the truth. Since she discovered this fact, she has taken action. In face-to-face inter-actions, Natalie deliberately controls her tone of voice, hand and body movements, and facial expressions. This way, her disposition is not distracting or does not get in the way of the message she's trying to convey. In stressful situations, she does the same thing. She remains even-keeled and doesn't jump to conclusions or plot the next course of action before all the facts are known. She listens to explanations and takes a few minutes before responding.

For Laurie, the focus of self-management is on reining in her intensity. Although she embraces it and deems it as an asset (as it has enabled her to achieve much success in both the entrepreneurial and corporate worlds and has motivated others to do the same), she also recognizes that it can be overwhelming for those she works with. She considers feedback as her "breakfast of champions" and constantly seeks it from peers and others in her community. Talking through circumstances in which she needs help allows her to adjust her interpersonal style and perform at the highest level possible.

Remember: There's no wrong type of personality—all types are valid and valuable. Continually managing that personality is key to improving your interpersonal style, expanding your influence, and cultivating your leadership style.

WHEN WEAVING WORK AND LIFE IS BETTER THAN BALANCING THEM

When we were just starting our careers, one of the biggest workplace trends was work–life balance, the idea that employees (especially working mothers) could nurture a career and a family in equal measure. Later on, the trend became life–work balance, the notion that employees value more time off to spend with their friends and family than more money. Today, a version of each trend still exists, but more and more they are being replaced by the question, is there such a thing as balance?

Balance implies that you are forcing two separate entities to cooperate with each other, to give and to take as necessary. In reality, neither life nor work is a good sharer. One always demands more than the other, and often both demand so much at the same time. Then, if one doesn't relent to the other, you could end up damaging both. That's not at all a comforting scenario.

A new paradigm has emerged that asks, why not accept that the two entities are woven together (or integrated) and that one doesn't end when the other begins? That's a self-aware perspective. It recognizes that work and life are not the same, but they are not separate, either. After all, who among us has not checked or responded to a work e-mail during our day off? And who among us has not made a personal phone call during work hours?

As you manage your work and life activities, keep your priorities straight and make adjustments as you see fit. Don't stress out if some of your activities overlap, because they often will. For example, a specific project—like a month-end or year-end strategic planning or budget forecasting—may consume or obligate you substantially. This might occur at the same time and clash with a life event, like the birth of a baby, the death or illness of a loved one, or a preparation for a wedding. These seasons or stages of life may cause you to lean more heavily into or away from your work obligations, but eventually things go back to normal.

The balancing method calls for compartmentalizing work and life into their own corners. If you were trying to balance, you might likely miss or not be involved in either a work or a personal event because you might think, "Personal time shouldn't encroach on work time, and vice versa." That's not realistic, and it causes an imbalance every day (ironically enough) because you become preoccupied with that thing you are not supposed to be doing anymore after a certain time (e.g., completing a departmental analysis) so that you can't focus on the thing you are supposed to be doing at present (e.g., going to the gym). In this age of the Internet, telecommuting, social networking, smartphones, and innovative living and working arrangements, it makes more sense to integrate than to separate the professional and the personal (see Schawbel 2014).

Weaving life into work and vice versa is not new; many people have been doing it for years. It's just that we hadn't given it a name yet and maybe we had been doing it all wrong. Having said that, the essential idea of a balanced life is still good. By "balanced," we mean the personal should be given the same value and respect as the professional (and vice versa), and adjustments should be made to allow for one priority to overtake the other when necessary.

The Personal Cost of Professional Success

James Andrews, MD, is an American orthopedic surgeon renowned for his expert skills, success rate, and his significant contributions to the field of sports medicine. He has been a sought-after surgeon for both amateur and professional athletes; among his star patients were Michael Jordan, Drew Brees, and Jack Nicklaus. He helped found the Andrews Institute (where he still practices at age 72) and the American Sports Medicine Institute (which churns out research about sports injuries and treatments). He introduced to his field some of the most innovative surgical and rehabilitation technologies still in use today (Helyar 2007). He has mentored up-and-coming orthopedists, has written a book, and gives motivational speeches.

By all accounts, he is on his cell phone when he's not consulting with patients or in the operating room. He fields calls not only from patients and their families but also from trainers, team owners, other orthopedic surgeons, physical therapists, and coaches (just to name a few). He makes himself available 24/7; in fact, always being available is one of his trademarks. And his productivity is legendary: At his peak, he performed 1,200 surgeries in one year, while the average orthopedist does about 400 annually (Eden 2013).

Dr. Andrews is likely envied by many. He's smart. He's accomplished. He's loved by those he has helped and continues to help. He's powerful and well connected. He's a one-of-a-kind asset to his field. From outside appearances, he has it all—much like so many whom people aspire to be and measure their achievements against. But what these comparisons tend *not* to show are the "personal sacrifices" made and the price tag attached to achieve a tremendous amount of success. (For Dr. Andrews, one trade-off was a heart attack in 2006.)

When you reflect on your own American dream, consider the trade-offs (and there will always be some):

- What are you giving up now? What will you be willing to give up later?
- What are you getting in return now? What do you expect to get in return later?
- Is the dream worth pursuing at the expense of everything else?

- When you look back on your life, will you have any regrets? Why, or why not?

Your answers to these questions (and feel free to come up with more) can guide you in managing your work and life priorities today. In addition, remember to consider the seasons of life. Freedom to invest in both personal and professional pursuits will ebb and flow as you go through those seasons.

WHAT WOULD A LIFELONG LEARNER DO?

Personal and professional development does not have to be expensive or over the top, like enrolling in a leadership immersion program for a month. It could be small and free but ongoing, like asking for feedback, interviewing an inspirational leader, using your commute to listen to audiobooks or podcasts, and staying connected with your network. These—and other such investments—pay off in various ways. Lifelong learning is not just informative; it also strengthens relationships, offers opportunities for change, enhances interpersonal skills, and reveals lasting lessons.

If you are a lifelong learner, you

- are disciplined (so that you can stick with development throughout your career),
- are curious (so that you never stop asking questions and finding answers), and
- have the right attitude (so that you can always be supportive of and enthusiastic about learning).

A self-aware person with a goal of becoming a lifelong learner would devise and follow a plan for cultivating her discipline, curiosity, and positive attitude. Plus, she would try the following methods.

Ask for Feedback

We meet a lot of professionals struggling in one or more skill areas. When we recommend that they ask for feedback, they almost always look like they just heard the definitive answer to "What's the meaning of life?" Although they aren't strangers to the idea of feedback, they've never solicited it and never thought it could help get them out of their bind. But oh yes, it can! Let us count the ways:

1. *The act of asking gets you out of the mind-set that you're on your own.* It is your unspoken (and maybe subconscious) acknowledgment that you are surrounded by people who care about your welfare. Plus, people feel honored to be asked for their honest opinions; that endears you to them.

2. *Feedback yields significant objective and subjective information.* Sift through the advice and pick out what could work for your situation. Take the criticisms seriously but not defensively; correct the wrongs, and don't attack the messengers. Be grateful for the compliments, and remind yourself of them when you feel doubtful about your talents and abilities.

3. *Feedback points you to some kind of direction.* That path may not be clear yet, but it eases your worries that you'll be stuck in one place. In other words, feedback gives you materials that you can turn into an improvement or a development plan, and it's all up to you to follow it.

4. *The entire process humbles you.* Asking for, receiving, and analyzing feedback—whether you do it in person or across a computer screen—can bruise the ego (especially if the ego belongs to an overly confident person). This is not a bad thing because it helps you develop a thick skin for the greater, badder ego-busting challenges you'll encounter later in your career.

People are almost always willing to help, so give them a chance to do so. Ask your mentor, boss, significant other, coworkers, past and current teachers, real-life friends, social media friends, parents, siblings, and anyone you have meaningful contact with on a regular basis. Don't be afraid that they'd say "yes"; be afraid that they'd say "no," because it means you'd miss out on a chance to learn.

Interview an Inspirational Leader

No, you didn't study journalism. But you don't need to be a reporter to have a question-and-answer session with a leader you admire. This leader doesn't have to be an executive working in a healthcare facility (although do approach these executives); it could be the chair of your health administration program, the head of a private quality-improvement organization, a physician or nurse leader, a member or chair of a hospital board, a new colleague you met at ACHE's Congress or in your local ACHE chapter, or any other remarkable individuals in your (presumably healthcare) workplace or field.

This interview doesn't have to be formal; it could take place over coffee or lunch, e-mail, or the phone. You could schedule it for one hour once a month, so that's at least 12 solid hours of learning per year. Be honest with the leaders about your intentions (e.g., you'd like to learn from their experiences, successes, and mistakes and to hear their insights). And assure them that you will not publish, post, or leak notes from your conversation (but if you were to do so, you will ask their permission).

Yes, we understand your invitation may be declined because leaders are typically very busy and may not be comfortable sharing details of their life with a stranger. But try anyway. The experience of reaching out to someone inspirational is, on its own, educational.

Stay Connected with Your Network

If you're like many people, you probably do this: (1) Attend an industry event (like ACHE's Congress on Healthcare Leadership), a seminar, or an alumni reunion; (2) see old friends and colleagues, and meet other professionals; (3) exchange business cards and promise to stay in touch; and (4) forget about the whole thing. No harm done, right? Not exactly.

When you're new to a field, you have to put extra effort into maintaining (not just building) a professional network. You shouldn't just collect business cards and handshakes. You should start conversations and keep them going. Here's one way to do that:

Every week, e-mail one colleague in your network just to check in and get to know the person more. Ask how he or she is doing, give a brief update about your life when appropriate (don't make the e-mail about you), and refer to something you discussed last time as that could still be a concern you could help with. Don't ask a favor from your contacts each time you reach out; in fact, don't ask a favor for a long time. That's the fastest way to lose them and to develop a reputation for being opportunistic and needy. (Note that these suggestions still apply if you call, text, snail mail, G-chat, or tweet instead of e-mail. Learn your connections' preferred media, and let them know yours.) Once you've established rapport, you may begin to recommend someone in your network whom you think your colleague would find value in getting to know. Share an article you've read that might be insightful or that will add value to their work, or congratulate them when you hear of their accomplishment. And voilà, you're functioning as a true networker!

Your network is a great source for many things, including feedback and recommendations for leaders you could interview. And so is your mentor, with whom you should definitely retain a connection. To express your appreciation for all the lessons and time the mentor has freely shared with you, you should write a thank you note to that person regularly (e.g., several times a year). In addition, you could invite your mentor to join you in educational activities, like listening to a podcast of interest to you both, attending an industry lecture or seminar, and reading and discussing a book or two. This way, you're not only spending quality time but also learning together.

Go Green, Stay Green

Dr. Andrews imparts some great wisdom for physicians and non-physicians alike. One of our favorites is, "If you're green, you're growing—and if you're ripe, you're next to rotten." This is meant to remind emerging leaders like you that you are in the right place and that your newness is an asset because it keeps you open for learning, maturing, evolving, and improving. Although you may have just the basic level of knowledge, skills, and abilities necessary (but not yet the instincts and mastery that come from years of practice), you have the desire and hunger to learn. Don't underestimate that.

In contrast, Dr. Andrews warns you of the decline that many (but not all!) seasoned professionals feel. By "rotten," he doesn't mean that these people are actually bad; he's just saying they have lost their sense of wonder, enthusiasm, and passion for their profession. They are now just carrying out their day-to-day duties to protect the status and income level they've earned. But they have stopped developing themselves, and they likely haven't been self-aware for decades.

Going green, in other words, is an analogy for stoking that fire inside you for learning and growth. Anyone can go green; it's not related to age, job title, or level of experience. Self-aware leaders work hard to stay green and promote the idea to their staffers, protégés, and colleagues.

So stay green! How? The answers are all over this book.

Remember These

- When you manage yourself, you are policing your own behavior and adjusting it to attain a desired outcome.
- Self-management is applied by many individuals, groups, and industries to many types of goals and objectives.
- Self-management involves choices, and those choices are influenced by self-awareness.
- Your personality is part of the many factors that make people want to engage with or disengage from you. That personality comes across in your interactions, so managing how you are perceived is important.
- The personal should be given the same value and respect as the professional (and vice versa), and adjustments should be made to allow for one priority to overtake the other when necessary.
- Lifelong learning is not just informative; it also strengthens relationships, offers opportunities for change, enhances interpersonal skills, and reveals lasting lessons.
- When you reflect on your own American dream, consider the trade-offs between professional success and personal happiness as well as the seasons in life.

REFERENCES

Eden, S. 2013. "The Doctor Will See You Now." *ESPN*. Posted September 17. http://espn.go.com/espn/story/_/id/9669812/celebrated-orthopedist-james-andrews-treats-robert-griffin-iii-bryce-harper-espn-magazine.

Helyar, J. 2007. "Dr. James Andrews Still Works on the Cutting Edge." *ESPN*. Posted September 20. http://sports.espn.go.com/espn/news/story?id=3024046.

Schawbel, D. 2014. "Work Life Integration: The New Norm." *Forbes*. Posted January 21. www.forbes.com/sites/danschawbel/2014/01/21/work-life-integration-the -new-norm/.

ADDITIONAL RESOURCE

Chappelow, C. 2012. "Strive for Work–Life Integration, Not Balance." *Fast Company*. www.fastcompany.com/1825042/strive-work-life-integration-not-balance.

Note to My 25-Year-Old Self

As I consider advice that might have helped me early in my career, much comes to mind. It is more than simply telling myself, "you just don't know how much you don't know." Often, people say they wish they knew that when they started. The reality is, you have decent book knowledge, just not much experience. The most valuable input I can share includes learning to listen well, live fearlessly, care for people, protect your home life, and be a person of great integrity.

Listen more . . . listen WAY more! Ask questions about people and their jobs and the implications of their clinical and operational decisions. Ask them why they chose healthcare. Find out what they like and don't like and how you can make things better. Listen to what they say and how they say it. Listen to what is not said. Observe. Probe. Learn.

When looking for work, interview that organization as well. Ask good questions. Listen carefully to the responses. Look for a boss and a culture that reflect your core values and an employer who cares about you and your career. Be prepared for the interview— not just for the questions you think they will ask you but also for the questions you will ask them. Give thought to the kinds of answers you expect and want to hear. It will tell you a lot about the people and culture. Err on the side of formality, not informality.

Live fearlessly! Don't be afraid of taking risks or making mistakes. We learn from mistakes, and you will never accomplish great things without taking risks. If you don't agree with a policy, a program, a direction, or a decision, challenge it. Do it respectfully, at an appropriate time, and in the appropriate place or setting, but do it! Don't accept the status quo just because it is easy or the cultural norm. Don't be afraid to push back. Also, don't be afraid of losing your job. Living and working in fear is counterproductive and unhealthy. If you lose your job because you disagree or challenge the leadership, it probably wasn't the right organization or job anyway. There are always other jobs for bright, talented, energetic, and hardworking young leaders.

People are more important than the tasks they do each day. Take time to get to know the employees and the physicians. Never forget that they are people first; they are moms and dads and husbands and wives and sisters and brothers and friends. They have hobbies and lives outside of work. Without being intrusive, get to know something about them that is not work-related. Ask questions; show genuine interest in your team. Again, listen, observe, care.

Go home. The work will always be there tomorrow. Family may not be. Home life needs to be your most important priority, and if things are going well at home, they will usually be good at work. If you are single, it is still important to go home, get away, and leave work behind. Take vacations—real vacations where you don't check e-mail and stay on the phone half the time. Work will go on without you! Really! By the way, this advice not only applies to you but to your people as well. Create an environment where you encourage your team to keep home as their most important priority. There are no winners in the illusion of a contest for who works the longest days or the most hours!

You already know this, but character counts more than anything else. Ask yourself important questions about your own behavior. Are you reliable? Can others count on you to do what you say you will do and when you say you will do it? Are you characterized as one who has a good work ethic and demonstrates honesty in all situations? Do you talk about others behind their back other than to praise them? Finally, make sure there are members of your team who will hold you accountable by telling you what you *need* to hear and not what you *want* to hear.

There is some obvious stuff for leaders that should not go unsaid. Ethical behavior must always come before all else—never sacrifice integrity. Provide service to others without self-interest—service above self. And finally, whatever you do, do it with excellence—always do your best!

Now go serve others, and have a blast! Healthcare is the greatest career. It's not a job, it's not even just a career; to those who lose themselves in it, it's a calling.

Signed,
Donald R. Avery, FACHE
President and CEO, Fairview Park Hospital

CHAPTER 3

Pay Attention to Your Character

*"Leadership is a potent combination of strategy and character.
But if you must be without one, be without strategy."*

—*General Norman Schwarzkopf, Jr., Former Commander
in Chief, US Central Command*

Reading Points

- Integrity

- Honesty and Trustworthiness

- Accountability

- Credibility

- How to Strengthen Character

IF A BILLIONAIRE wrote you a $1 million check to spend how-
ever you like, how would you treat that check? Would you hold it
between your fingers all day long, pass it around to show it off, or
leave it unguarded on your desk? Would you risk losing or damaging it? Now consider how you treat something much more valuable
than $1 million: your character, something no one can steal from

you but demands more vigilance and protection because ruining it has far greater consequences than destroying a check. Do you pay your character as much attention as you would a huge sum? Do you realize it's equally life changing?

Character is not just a word. It's the entire package of a person's personality, moral and ethical beliefs, motivation, attitude, behavior, thinking and speaking patterns, and so much more. The *Merriam-Webster Dictionary* defines it as the "way someone thinks, feels, and behaves." Simply, your character is how those who know you describe your essence to those who don't know you. It's part of your personal brand. (See Chapter 5 for more discussion on this.)

Of these definitions, the behavior part is, for us, the most important. Why? Because your conduct—including your words—is what people see, feel, interact with, listen and respond to, mimic, and judge. Ultimately, it is every aspect of your actions done repeatedly over time (and not your intentions, thoughts, feelings, or plans—no matter how noble they are) that defines your character in people's minds.

For example, if we say we're committed to our career or organization but consistently miss deadlines, produce sloppy work, don't carry ourselves with decorum, or don't attend events or meetings that contribute to our growth, our behavior shows us to be unreliable at best but untrustworthy at worst. And our reasons for not being able to deliver on our promise? Our bosses don't want to hear those. How about our new pledge to be better? They *really* don't want to hear that.

So watch what you do and what you say at all times. Better yet, be aware of the character (or personality) traits that drive you to behave a certain way. Because as we've said in earlier chapters, knowing your true self is the first step to managing yourself. And the more you manage your character, the more you develop desirable traits, the better you can manage others' perception of you, and the wider you can expand your influence.

In this chapter, we discuss integrity, the building block of good character. It includes the traits of honesty, trustworthiness, accountability, and credibility. These traits are interrelated and build on each other; that is, if you have integrity, you're honest; if you're honest, you're trustworthy; if you're trustworthy, you're accountable; and if you're accountable, you're credible. Here, we also offer tips for properly delivering an apology, caution about practices that could diminish credibility, and strategies for developing character.

But before we get started, let's be clear on several things.

First, character development—just like any kind of growth—can be arduous. It requires commitment and self-discipline. (See Chapter 4 for more on these concepts.) It requires you to abandon the comfort zone, the status quo, or the business as usual. No one else—not us, not your professors, not your mentors, not your bosses, not your peers and coworkers, and not your fairy godmother—but *you* can make that choice or do that work for you. Given that you're reading this book, we think you've made the right choice for your career!

Second, don't wait until you're a titled leader (like a CEO, COO, or VP) to develop the character-driven qualities that would set you apart from the rest. Start today, if you didn't do it yesterday. Even if your career path or interest changes later, the time and effort you invest in character building will *always* be personally and professionally rewarded. If you're not an early careerist and are already leading people and departments, don't get discouraged and think you're now too set in your ways to make adjustments. It's never too late for course correction or to nurture better habits—regardless of age, job title or level, experience, or industry. Been there, done that? We say, keep doing it!

Third, paying attention to your character is not a one-time process but a lifetime pursuit. It may feel like "two steps forward, one step back" from time to time. That's natural. Recovery, learning from it, and applying the lesson to future behavior is part of the process. The different seasons or stages of life—from being a student and single, to having a full-time career and married with or without children, to being a retiree—tend to alter some of your character traits. Who you are in your twenties and thirties may not be exactly who you are in your fifties and sixties. Be self-aware enough to notice the differences as you get older and encounter new experiences.

INTEGRITY

Selling out or betraying deeply held convictions for power, monetary gain, or some other benefit. Saying one thing but doing another. Running away from adversity and leaving everyone else to deal with the mess. Lying, misleading, withholding information, blaming someone else, or participating in a cover up to avoid the consequences of a wrong decision. Associating with or supporting people who are unethical or get involved in illegal activities. Cheating and committing fraud. These are just some of the behaviors displayed by those who lack integrity. Consider the integrity breaches by "successful" people—from athletes (e.g., professional cyclist Lance Armstrong) to sports coaches (e.g., former Ohio State University football head coach Jim Tressel) to finance titans (e.g., Bernie Madoff) to healthcare administrators (e.g., presidents and CEOs convicted of Medicare fraud and abuse or other legal violations). At the end of the day, no amount of wealth, monumental accomplishments, and brilliant skills were enough to save these people from their unscrupulous character. So, sure, lacking integrity doesn't stop anyone from attaining their dreams, but it also doesn't help anyone keep living those dreams.

Integrity is the catch-all word for being truthful, fair, honorable, ethical, responsible, kind and caring, conscientious, faithful or loyal, and unselfish. In other words, if you have integrity, you do the right thing—all the time, no matter what, regardless of whether anyone is watching. This doesn't mean you always live up to expectations or you don't ever make mistakes. We all make mistakes, of course! But it means you handle each misstep or challenging situation with honesty, humility, consideration of and respect for others' thoughts and feelings, and desire to make things right again. This last point is especially critical because it is about rebuilding trust, the topic of discussion in the next section.

There's no better way to illustrate these concepts than to tell a story, so we share here a true event that happened to Laurie about half a decade ago.

Laurie's Apology[1]

I was working on a project with a group of surgeons, a client with whom I have been privileged to work for nearly a decade. Our relationship dynamic is one filled with significant trust and mutual respect. We have lived through an inordinate amount of dysfunction and some unique and harrowing events.

At one point, when I felt that a decision we were leaning toward as a group was not the right one, I took the latitude to go a different direction. Let me clarify: This was not an operational decision. It did not have significant financial or organizational impact. It was a vendor selection, to be exact.

The group had reached a stalemate in making a decision, mostly due to a personal connection one of the physician-owners had to one of the vendors being considered. In the end, I chose to contract with an alternate vendor, veering away from those we had previously discussed.

When I made this decision, I believed (and still believe) it to be in the best interests of the group. I also knew, without a doubt, that it was going to cause a rift between the physician and me. Taking those factors into consideration, I still moved forward. I alerted the external parties involved, finalized arrangements, and then notified the client of my actions.

As predicted, the physician became very upset. I lost a lot of her trust.

I had built an account of trust with this group, penny by penny and over a number of years. But my decision took a sizable withdrawal from that account. It took a few weeks for the palpable tension between us to wear away and another several months for our relationship to regain the easy stride it once had. Now, five years later, that event is thankfully a distant memory. But it will always be a distinct learning experience for me.

So how did I come back from that? Slowly but surely, with these simple but powerful acts:

1. *Apologize.* What do you do when you mess up? Do what your mother taught you and say you're sorry. We are not perfect beings, so we make mistakes; those mistakes don't end at some magical point in our career! But no matter how much we err, we shouldn't be too proud to acknowledge our shortcomings and take responsibility for the hurt or damage we caused. It's never fun to do so, but it's always worth the effort because it reopens the path to communication. (See Exhibit 3.1 for further discussion on apology.)

    A brief e-mail exchange followed my original notification to the client, and it was very clear then that the physician was not happy with what I had done. I knew the group's personality and communication style, so I thought it best to apologize in person. Approaching the physicians the next morning to apologize face to face was definitely not the easiest thing to do. It was scary! But I knew I needed to show my respect for each of them by looking them in the eye, taking responsibility for my actions, and explaining the thought process behind my decision.

    I didn't apologize because I did something without my client's approval. Again, I still believe my decision was the most appropriate given the circumstances we were in. I apologized because my actions compromised their trust in me. I admitted that I would work diligently to regain their trust and restore our relationship, and apologizing was only the first step.

2. *Be humble.* Humility is the natural companion to apology and thus is an essential and nonnegotiable trait of a leader with strong character. If you maintain a humbled approach, you're sending a message that you want to learn and improve from the incident and the other party's respect for you grows.

My apology to my client was sincere and humble. Even my written and face-to-face explanations conveyed the tone of my regret. I wasn't defensive or trying to cover up my error; instead, I based my actions on fact and the desire to be helpful. My goal was to walk my client through the steps from beginning to end, without creating a chasm between us. I listened to what they had to say with deference, humbled by their generosity of spirit and the fact that they were willing to give me another chance. This was a valuable learning experience for me. It was a lesson in humility, decision making, and interpersonal relationships all wrapped up into one.

3. *Be honest.* Even in simple situations, it is far better to admit you don't know the answer than to make something up. Politely decline to comment, if you must. But don't engage in a conversation you aren't comfortable having and then dance around the subject because you lack information. Most important, never attempt to cover your tracks. The truth always comes out. The temptation to be dishonest—even if it temporarily lessens the heat on you—is never the right choice.

During the brief e-mail exchange following the original notification, the physicians asked me several direct questions about what transpired and how I handled certain communications. At least one of those messages was forwarded to other parties, to cross-check or verify my version of the events. Had I not been honest from the start, the situation would have gone from challenging to relationship ending.

HONESTY AND TRUSTWORTHINESS

"Trust is earned a penny at a time and spent in dollar bills." This is a point Laurie makes each time she speaks to grad students and emerging leaders about trust. Essentially, it means that trust takes months and years to build but a minute to demolish (although

---

Exhibit 3.1 The Art of the Apology

Why is it so hard to apologize? Let's count the reasons:

1. *We're embarrassed.* A mistake of any kind is blush inducing and ego bruising. Apologizing for it only magnifies the error made.
2. *We're afraid to look incompetent.* Would we be seen as weak or not good enough? And if that is the perception, then would it cost us our job, undermine our previous excellent performance, or take away our chances for a promotion?
3. *We're afraid of the risks.* What comes after the apology in which we admit to be wrong? Are we legally liable for the fallout? Would it ruin our reputation, our good name? Would it make us a target of jokes, hostility, or retaliation?

   Despite these reasons and the high stakes, we have to do the right thing. An apology

   • acknowledges the issue, and presents an opportunity to right a wrong;
   • shows we're human with integrity and humility; and
   • starts to restore a damaged relationship.

The qualities of a good apology include the following:

1. *Timely.* Waiting too long is disrespectful. But apologizing too soon doesn't give the receiving party time to react to what happened and thus could prevent them from even processing the apology.

(continued)

2. *Genuine.* This goes without saying: Don't fake tears, sympathy, empathy, remorse, and other markers of regret and sorrow. That is insulting to the receiving party and is obvious.
3. *Specific.* Address the specific wrongdoing head on.
4. *Personal.* Approach the other party yourself—no middlemen or messengers allowed. The more personal the delivery is, the better. A face-to-face meeting or a handwritten note always wins over an e-mail or a phone call.
5. *Accountable.* Own up to the wrong, don't pass blame, and don't make excuses.
6. *Educational.* No one is ever too old, too young, too low level, or too high level to learn from mistakes, painful experiences, or an uncomfortable apology process and to strive not to repeat them. Learning from the event is the most valuable component of an apology.

Notice that people who are not self-aware and who don't self-reflect tend not to apologize. Is it because of their big egos? Is it because they are so blind to what's going on around them that they don't even see the need for an apology? Many of them who do manage to issue an "apology" commit the most counterproductive offenses: (1) pretend the incident never happened, (2) pass the blame, (3) lie, and (4) get defensive.

Master the art of the apology. Because we all make mistakes, it will only be a matter of time until you have to rely on this valuable skill.

---

a new school of "instant trust" has emerged; see Stephen M. R. Covey's book mentioned in Chapter 1, for example). This lesson is evident not only in Laurie's story about her clients but also in Natalie's experiences when she became the new CEO of an established hospital with an existing staff and an involved community (a story shared in a later chapter). We also both live by this principle of earning and maintaining trust. How? We conduct ourselves with integrity and approach everything with honesty.

Honesty is not just about telling the truth. It is also about meaning what you say, following through on promises and commitments, presenting the authentic you (not some pretend version of you), being candid but constructive with your criticism or feedback, not giving false hopes or perceptions by sugarcoating a bad situation, admitting your faults and errors, and practicing transparency. Each time you do something you said you would do (like making a phone call to someone you promised to contact, for example), you are dropping a coin into the other party's trust piggy bank. Each time you share information that would help others improve their job performance or self-understanding, you are dropping a coin into that bank. A lie—even a tiny one—could immediately empty out that trust bank. In other words, honesty (not to mention integrity) is the fastest way you can build or break trust.

When you gain people's trust through honesty, they view you as reliable, respectable, accountable, and credible.

ACCOUNTABILITY

We're sure you've heard the phrases "take responsibility for your actions" and "the buck stops here" and "be part of the solution, not the problem." They all mean the same thing: Be accountable.

Accountability begins with taking ownership of _____ (fill in the blank)—be it a project or assignment, your career trajectory, or your behavior. When you take ownership of a project, for example, you are not merely the person who does your part day in and day out but you are also the person who pushes yourself to do your part correctly and on time. The words "not my job" or "I didn't do it" or I'm on lunch" are not in your vocabulary. You often volunteer to help other team members, and you're honored when someone comes to you for help or advice. You're the first to report your own error in hopes that you could stop it from doing further damage. You admit when you're wrong, don't make excuses but are clear about the reasons, and face consequences graciously. You find finger pointing ridiculous and punishment unproductive; instead, you value problem solving and not wasting time. And you are master at being honest with yourself: When something goes wrong, you do a self-assessment to figure out the part you played in the incident so that you don't repeat that gaffe next time. In a word, when you're accountable, you are committed to, enthusiastic about, and grateful for whatever opportunity or situation you are involved in.

Practicing accountability is not easy because not everything is within our control, and eschewing responsibility is tempting. But your deliberate efforts in this area not only elevate your reputation and add currency to your trust bank but also raise your credibility. The more you showcase that you are accountable, the more you convince others of your credibility—that you can do a job well and deliver great results.

CREDIBILITY

Credibility is a person's level of trustworthiness and believability. Like trust, credibility takes a long time to gain but a short time to lose (see Exhibit 3.2). And like trust, it requires maintenance. But unlike trust (which is often measured by the intangible like integrity and values), credibility is often measured by the tangible (like professional results, accomplishments, and specific skills).

Here's a shortlist of what makes someone credible:

- Academic or professional credentials
- Work experience
- Trustworthiness
- Transparency
- Accountability
- Strong judgment based on evidence and experience
- Project or organizational outcomes
- Critical thinking and decision-making skills
- Responsiveness and reliability
- Interpersonal abilities and emotional intelligence

- Team orientation
- Expert- or high-level competence
- Workplace and culture savvy
- Advanced social skills
- Focus on goals and results

Now, a word to the wise: Don't get bogged down in definitions. If you Google "difference between trust and credibility," you'll get millions of results, each seemingly contradicting the others. The important thing to remember is that trust and credibility go hand in hand; no book, article, blog post, or study discusses one without the other. Both are traits that convince people to have faith and confidence in someone's ability. A leader who has a superb character possesses both.

HOW TO STRENGTHEN CHARACTER

Ultimately, the major and minor actions you take regularly and deliberately define your character. The more you engage in good behavior, the more the behaviors become a habit. The deeper these

---

Exhibit 3.2 Eight Ways to Lose Credibility

1. Pass the blame, make up excuses, and don't take accountability for your actions.
2. Miss deadlines consistently, don't follow through, and manage time and priorities poorly.
3. Ignore discretion.
4. Overpromise and underdeliver.
5. Withhold information.
6. Participate in or initiate office or organizational gossip.
7. Play favorites.
8. Pursue or engage in inappropriate personal relationships with a coworker, a boss, a subordinate, or a contractor.

---

habits are engrained in you, the stronger your character and the better your responses become to any situation. Identify and then adopt behaviors that exemplify your character, and then embed those behaviors in your daily routine until they become habits.

Exhibit 3.3 presents character-building exercises that you can apply at home, in the office, and anyplace in between.

Exhibit 3.3 Character-Building Exercises

Many of these practices may test your patience and resolve or may feel awkward or feel like a chore. Those are the feelings you're supposed to have! As Helen Keller has been quoted as saying, "Character cannot be developed in ease and quiet. Only through experience of trial and suffering can the soul be strengthened, vision cleared, ambition inspired, and success achieved."

Manage Your Impulses

Do you interrupt or talk over others? Do you make side comments, read your social media feeds, type out texts or e-mails, or sigh and yawn audibly during meetings when you get bored or need attention? Do you talk incessantly about yourself to anyone—even complete strangers? Do you throw things, yell, curse, and storm out when you get upset? Do you dismiss people, call them names, or assign them derogatory nicknames? Do you often come in late, disheveled, and out of it; call in sick; and leave early? If so, are you aware of other people's reactions to you? Are you aware you need to change such behaviors? Why? Because they are untenable, disruptive, disconcerting, unprofessional, and even threatening. If you can't manage your own impulses, you can't be viewed as someone who can manage a staff. When you manage yourself, you are seen as someone who is ready and capable for the next level, someone who can gain people's respect, trust, loyalty, and support.

Invest in Yourself

Read books, volunteer your time and skills, listen to podcasts, follow thought leaders (not just anyone) on social media, go to lectures and seminars, travel, meet new people, try new experiences, take a night class. However you decide to invest in yourself, do it often—no matter how busy you get or how uncomfortable you are with the idea—because

(continued)

learning is about challenging yourself and getting to know you and so much more in the process. Don't wait for your organization to offer, require, or sponsor a formal continuing education session or program (which you shouldn't miss), but seek and make your own training—however unconventional or informal.

Acknowledge Others

So many people in a healthcare facility go unthanked because so much of the recognition is focused on the main players—the C-suite, the administrators, the board, the doctors, the nurses, and the other clinicians. But just like in the movies, the "bit players" don't often get acknowledged because their names are in very tiny print when the credits roll, so to speak. We mean the various support and maintenance staff whose hard work keeps the facility running smoothly. They deserve to be treated with kindness and respect and to be recognized as a matter of course. Thank them when you can, not just when they've done something for you. Don't ignore and make them feel invisible, disposable, or less important. Like you, they contribute to the greater goals of the organization. A simple "thank you," a nod, a hello, a smile, a quick chat, or just simply knowing their names would suffice. Leave the generous speeches and pizza parties to your bosses for now. Beyond this, always give credit where it's due. You've heard that all your life because it's excellent advice.

Practice Hope and Serenity

When you're hopeful, you imbue everything you do with optimism. And when you're optimistic, you tend to be less frazzled and think more clearly—especially in a constantly high-pressure environment like a hospital. And when you're calm amid turmoil, you tend to be perceived as an inspiration and worthy of respect (although people may think you're crazy at first). We know being calm and positive do not seem possible during staff shortages, sweeping layoffs, budget cuts, mergers, and major change initiatives. But the diligent trying alone will do so much to build your character and boost your own (and others') morale. Plus, "[r]esearch shows that when people work with a positive mind-set, performance on nearly every level—productivity, creativity, engagement—improves" (Achor 2012).

Remember These

- Character is the entire package of a person's personality, moral and ethical beliefs, motivation, attitude, behavior, thinking and speaking patterns, and so much more. It's how those who know you describe your essence to those who don't know you. It's part of your personal brand.

- Character development—just like any kind of growth—can be arduous. It requires commitment and self-discipline. It requires you to abandon the comfort zone, the status quo, or the business as usual.

- Don't wait until you're a titled leader to develop the character-driven qualities that would set you apart from the rest.

- Even if your career path or interest changes later, the time and effort you invest in character building will *always* be personally and professionally rewarded.

- Paying attention to your character is not a one-time process but a lifetime pursuit.

- If you have integrity, you do the right thing—all the time, no matter what, regardless of whether anyone is watching.

- Master the art of the apology. Because we all make mistakes, it will only be a matter of time until you have to rely on this valuable skill.

- Trust takes months and years to build but a minute to demolish.

- Practicing accountability is not easy because not everything is within our control, and eschewing responsibility is tempting. But your deliberate efforts in this area not only elevate your reputation and add currency to your trust bank but also raise your credibility.

$\longrightarrow$

- Unlike trust (which is often measured by the intangible, like integrity and values), credibility is often measured by the tangible (like professional results, accomplishments, and specific skills).
- Identify and then adopt behaviors that exemplify your character, and then embed those behaviors in your daily routine until they become habits.

NOTE

1. The original version of Laurie's story appeared at www .lauriebaedke.com/2011/02/07/trust-is-earned-a-penny-at-a -time-and-spent-in-dollar-bills/. Her story has been edited to fit the context of this chapter.

REFERENCE

Achor, S. 2012. "Positive Inteligence." *Harvard Business Review*. Accessed September 1. http://hbr.org/2012/01/positive-intelligence/ar/1.

ADDITIONAL RESOURCES

Adams, S. 2014. "Humble CEOs Are Best for Business, New Study Says." *Forbes*. www.forbes.com/sites/susanadams/2014/07/29/humble-ceos-are-best-for -business-new-study-says/.

Biro, M. 2012. "Are You a Character-Based Leader?" *Forbes*. www.forbes.com/sites /meghanbiro/2012/09/30/are-you-a-character-based-leader/.

Mixon, E. 2013. "Humility in the Workplace." www.hrtalentmanagement.com/2013 /12/11/humility-in-the-workplace/.

National Public Radio. 2013. "Tact, Tone, and Timing: The Power of Apology." *Talk of the Nation*. www.npr.org/2013/05/28/186922987/tact-tone-and-timing -the-power-of-apology.

Prime, J., and E. Salib. 2014. "The Best Leaders Are Humble Leaders." *Harvard Business Review* Blog Network. http://blogs.hbr.org/2014/05/the-best-leaders -are-humble-leaders/.

CHAPTER 4

Consciously Commit to and Exercise Self-Discipline

"It takes a deep commitment to change and
an even deeper commitment to grow."

—*Ralph Ellison, Novelist*

Reading Points

- Are You Up for Going All In?

- Why Mind the Little Things?

- What Should You Commit To?

- Strategic Commitment, Not Sacrifice

IF GIVEN A vague promise (I'll call you after the holidays) and a firm commitment (I'll call you on January 3), which would you believe? The former is typically an autopilot response—something you say or do without much thought. The latter, on the other hand, is mindful, intentional, or deliberate—something you've carefully considered and planned. Which group do you belong in?

If you're self-aware, if you practice self-management, and if you pay attention to your character and live with integrity, then you are equipped not only to make a conscious commitment but also to exercise self-discipline. That is to say, you can push yourself, committing to ever-higher goals and then persevering through the inevitable challenges. This combination of commitment and self-discipline (which is every bit a part of your personal brand) applies to everything you do—whether you're training for a grueling 26.2-mile marathon, implementing unpopular or difficult policies and processes, pursuing a certification or an advanced degree, or learning to blend well with the culture of a new organization. Plus, it is an indicator of how strong your work ethic is.

When you commit, you are sending the signal to *everybody* that you are ready for the good, the bad, the ugly, and the unexpected. More important, when you commit, you are sending the signal to *yourself* to use all the resources, techniques, and abilities at your disposal that enable you to deliver on your promise.

In this chapter, we offer practical strategies for helping you commit and apply self-discipline. We also cover the professional areas to which you should commit as well as present a different take on *sacrifice*, the term often associated with commitment.

ARE YOU UP FOR GOING ALL IN?

If you commit, you have to go all in. And if you go all in, you have to let your conscious mind take over. There are multiple ways to deliberately commit. Here are just a few:

- *Evaluate your psyche.* Why do you want to commit? What motivates or drives you? How determined are you? Are you willing to push through doubt, resistance, setback, complications, lack of support, time constraints, exhaustion, pain, illness, hunger, laziness, bad weather, great weather, and anything else that could impede your progress? Do you have enough self-discipline to follow through on plans? Are you a quitter, a finisher, a watcher, or a doer? Which of your character traits will help or hinder you? Self-evaluation should always be the first step in any pursuit, especially a demanding one such as making a commitment. Beyond probing your own psyche, talk to others who know you well. Ask to find out, then listen to learn.

- *Set specific goals—a big one and several little ones.* What do you want to accomplish? When? How? If you get stuck on the details of how, break the big goal down into small but doable parts. For example, if your big goal is to become the director of patient care services two years after earning an MHA, then your small goals may be finding out the qualifications of the position, honing the relevant skills you already have through on-the-job practice, and acquiring the required skills and experiences through formal and informal education or training. Every goal is a plural; it's composed of many singular objectives, each of which has multiple steps with differing aims. So when you set a goal, make it as unambiguous as possible. The clearer you are, the better you can articulate a multilayered vision and plan. That detailed goal can be intimidating to pursue, but consider it one of the early tests of your commitment and self-discipline.

- *Make a plan.* Without a plan for how to realize the commitment, you could get sidetracked and quit. Like setting goals, making a plan has to be specific. Specifics may include the steps, time frame, tools and resources, and desired outcomes for each objective and goal. The more details you include, the better your chances of following through on those details (because you don't have to do any guesswork; everything is already laid out). And before you know it, you are living the plan!

- *Track your progress.* If you committed to losing weight, don't you jump on the scale every once in a while to see whether you're shedding pounds? If you committed to saving money, don't you check your bank balance to see if it's growing? The same idea applies when you commit to professional development, for example. Only this time, the measures you use are the feedback from others and the outcomes you've delivered since you first committed to improve. Good or bad or stagnant, the results are informative and could encourage you to try harder or more consciously if you want better outcomes.

- *Make time for what matters.* You designate a time for everything that matters to you, so why not allocate time to allow your commitment to take hold? And the time your commitment requires doesn't necessarily have to further complicate or crowd your schedule. Practicing new methods or applying new concepts happens on your feet, or they replace old ones that have become inefficient or ineffective, so they don't take up extra time. And when you scrutinize how you spend your hours during the day, evening, week, and weekend, you likely will find free time for more productive activities. Don't be a cliché and use "too busy" as an excuse; be an original and do the unexpected—make time and make that time count.

WHY MIND THE LITTLE THINGS?

All of the strategies we recommend here and in other chapters can be done in increments—a little at a time. There's no set time limit to personal and professional development, and certainly no one is expecting you to completely transform yourself overnight. Many of these strategies take a lifetime to master anyway. Plus, setbacks happen that could undo your progress. So it only makes sense to take a little-by-little approach.

Self-discipline, much like other character traits, develops one small act at a time. Here's how:

- *Start and finish one task.* Select a task that is simple but not inconsequential or lowest priority, and then set a deadline (i.e., do it for a certain amount of time—like one hour or half a day). Don't let anyone or anything interrupt you (unless, of course, an emergency pops up). Don't think about your other projects. Don't dwell on how many other "better" things you could be doing. Just concentrate on finishing within the deadline. The point of this exercise is threefold: (1) to get you to practice restraint or control your impulse to multitask (which, by the way, is a myth and breeds poor performance because realistically the brain can process only one stimulant at a time), (2) to give you a chance to fully and satisfyingly handle one activity or problem, and (3) to get you to push away thoughts and feelings that weaken your concentration or resolve.

- *Treat yourself.* If you're like us, your work lunch is quick and uneventful; that means no chocolate mousse topped with a swirl of candied fruit or whipped cream for dessert! The things that you enjoy but deprive yourself of—be it dessert, TV time, or some other indulgence—are the very things that you can use as rewards for all your efforts. Self-discipline should not be 24/7 of work and control; it should also be interspersed with celebrations and down time. The breaks and treats you give yourself represent a pat on the back, gratitude for doing something, an encouragement to continue, and an acknowledgement of the effort—win or lose, goals achieved or not. That's what you'd give to someone else when he has worked so hard and so consistently, right? When you allow yourself the same courtesy, you'll find your mind refreshed and your commitment renewed.

- *Choose carefully.* Admit it: If given five free hours and a choice between watching your favorite show and reading a development book, you'd likely pick the former. That's cool; it's your five hours, after all. But when you consider the time you're devoting to that activity versus the benefits you're gaining from it, you might have second thoughts about that choice. That's the point of our argument: Self-discipline involves the ability to be more discerning about your choices and to remove yourself from tempting situations that might be enjoyable today but could hurt you in the future (Szalavitz 2013). So beware of choices that lead you to slack off. If that's not convincing enough, how about this: Warren Buffett doesn't choose to watch three hours of television every night.

- *Work through the difficulty.* Basketball legend Michael Jordan had the flu but still scored 38 points that led to a Chicago Bulls win during the 1997 NBA finals. *Harry Potter* author J. K. Rowling began writing the wildly popular series while she was on welfare, suffering from depression, and grieving her mother's death. While developing the first draft of this book, Natalie was undergoing onboarding for a new CEO role, while Laurie was immersed in guiding her organization through a merger. There are many more examples of people pushing through seemingly impossible situations and coming out victorious. What these examples tell us is that self-disciplined people don't use adversity, setbacks, and discomfort as an excuse. They persevere, despite their strong impulse to quit, postpone, or forget about the activity they committed to complete or be involved in.

All of these small acts may seem not a big deal or too simple to help you become more self-disciplined. But doing them consistently turns them into habits or automatic responses. In turn, the small things add up and result in huge changes in how you enter into a commitment and how you fulfill that commitment. Jeff Olson (2011, 30), author of the book *The Slight Edge*, talks about the value of improvement through small acts, saying:

> The things you do every single day, the things that don't look dramatic, that don't even look like they matter, do matter. That they not only make the difference—they make all the difference.

WHAT SHOULD YOU COMMIT TO?

We're not telling you what to commit to. That's your job and your choice. What we present in this section are some of the areas that you should commit to improving. Based on our experience, applying a disciplined approach in these areas could help you become the professional who, at least, gets considered for the next opportunity and who, at best, gets picked for the next job.

Constant Learning

We hear of an educational seminar or skill improvement training, and we're all ears. We experience a bad day or face a tough situation at work (and at home, too), and we're automatically asking ourselves what lessons we can take away so that we don't repeat it. We didn't get this way because our jobs required it. We didn't get this way because our colleagues or professors or superiors or mentors shamed us into being so. We're each naturally curious, and we're both compelled to become better people and better professionals. We committed to learning long before we decided on what career to pursue, and we never stopped. So for us, learning just became a habit, something we don't even think about.

Now let's talk about you.

Did you know job recruiters spend only six seconds to screen each resumé? And 80 percent of those six seconds are spent on just a few details, including education (Strom 2013)—that very same section in your resumé that contains not just your degrees but also continuing education or training credits, certifications, and other skill-improvement courses. So if you want a chance to get in a recruiter's or hiring manager's "yes" pile, beef up that section of your resumé.

Beyond what your career requires, you should commit to continual learning to improve you. Here's why:

1. It introduces you to innovative ideas, classic and new methods, trends, and different worlds and people. Sure, you might have heard or even studied some of these things in graduate school, but this type of exposure is hands-on and intended to be more applicable to your current responsibilities and goals. Even if you don't learn anything new (which is unlikely), you'll get a good refresher and come away with a different perspective.

2. It gives you an opportunity to network with a diverse group of professionals. Some of these contacts may remain in your life for a long time, serving as resources, business partners, sounding boards, mentors, teachers, or just plain-old friends.

3. It widens your view. When you're entrenched in one industry or field, you tend to stick to your kind, speaking the lingo and abiding by the same tried-and-true rules or principles as everyone else. There's nothing wrong with that at all. But do venture out of your own industry every so often to understand how others do their business, manage their staff and operations, and so on. By doing this, you can learn practices that are applicable or even essential to what you do day in and day out. Just look at the process and quality improvement tools that have been

adopted in healthcare like the Toyota Production System, Six Sigma, and Crew Resource Management (from the car, electronics, and aviation industries, respectively) or the term and concept of *customers* or *consumers* now applied to patients (from the for-profit sector and the marketing industry).

Thanks to the Internet and advancements in technology, constant learning is now easier than ever to commit to. There are YouTube and Vimeo channels, podcasts, blogs and vlogs, on-demand streaming, webinars, and audiobooks and e-books (which Laurie prefers) on top of the in-person lectures, seminars, conferences, and meetings (which Natalie prefers). Find out what format works best for you, pick a subject (if it's a one-topic, one-class arrangement) you are interested in or need to boost or acquire skills, devote the time to it, and sign up or attend. Beyond these, we also suggest reading management and leadership books written for a general audience. Check out books by Jim Collins, Patrick Lencioni, and John Maxwell, to name just a few.

If you continue to learn, you could become that rare person who is knowledgeable about a lot of things *and* an expert in one thing. That is an asset no one can take away from you.

Building Relationships

There are so many kinds and levels of relationships to be had in healthcare, and all of them are important. Your commitment in this area is not just about creating connections (through networking, mentorship, fellowship/internship, and normal business operations) but also nurturing and maintaining those connections by serving them.

We've mentioned before that your connections are a good resource. You may ask them to give you feedback, advice, support, opinions, and other business-related favors. But let us clarify that:

Do so only *after* establishing a rapport with them, and always focus on what you can do for or how you can serve them—not the other way around. Although almost every relationship ultimately yields a mutual benefit for the parties involved, the benefits shouldn't be the only reason you are forging a connection with someone. When you do gain some kind of benefit, pay it back by not letting down those who reached out to you or pay it forward by becoming a mentor or opening doors for someone else.

Committing to building relationships means the small acts of meeting new people, finding a commonality, getting to know each other over time, treating them with kindness and respect, calling or emailing once in a while to say hello or ask about their life, offering help without an expectation of a favor in return, sending handwritten notes and cards when appropriate, and even visiting when the other is in town. This kind of nurturing takes years— perhaps even decades. It's a true manifestation of self-discipline.

Even a mentor–mentee/protégé relationship requires some TLC. Mentors are not fairies who grant favors and make wishes come true. They are teachers and advisors, who dispense knowledge and insights—voluntarily. The wisdom and understanding you gain by listening to them are the cake and icing, so to speak; anything beyond that is decoration. They really don't owe you anything.

If you don't have a mentor, approach someone whose character, style, and achievements are admirable to you. If you do have a mentor, acknowledge that person's contributions to your growth and express your gratitude—not just once but regularly.

Asking for Help

It means admitting to your boss that you didn't understand the directives for your new assignment. It means getting verification straight from the source of information—even if that person is a member of the C-suite or the board—to ensure you don't end up wasting valuable resources. It means networking with like-minded professionals who are facing the same challenges as you are. It means accepting assistance from those who have more experience and knowledge.

What it *doesn't* mean (or shouldn't make you feel) is that you're incompetent or inadequate. In fact, asking for help is a sign that you're self-aware and open to opportunities and new ideas. It also shows you are so committed to your job and career that you're willing to go to great lengths to get things right. The flip side to not asking for help is isolation. Isolated—from learning, networking, and improvement opportunities—is perhaps one of the worst situations you'll find yourself in at any time, but especially when you're building a career.

Thinking Outside the Box

We know this is cliché, but don't discount it. Being innovative is not just for Silicon Valley. It pays off in other industries, too. Take, for example, the story of how Natalie found one of her mentors. Every Friday, her graduate program invited CEOs to come and speak to the students. Afterward, the students had an opportunity to come up to the CEO and ask follow-up questions. Natalie went beyond talking and shaking hands with the CEOs. She handed each of them her business card stapled to her resumé, introduced herself, and said: "Can I take you to lunch? Can I pick your brain?"

It was a bold move, but it didn't always yield the results she wanted. Although many CEOs said "yes," most of them never called. In fact, as she was leaving one of those sessions, she found her resumé with a business card in the trashcan—right outside the room! Disappointed, embarrassed, but not beaten, Natalie picked it up and continued her plan. After all, there were more Fridays to come and more CEOs to meet.

And then she met her future mentor, a well-known healthcare leader who has consistently been named as one of the 100 Most

Influential Leaders in Healthcare. When she gave this leader her quick spiel, he said "yes." She was overjoyed because she'd always admired him. And when his assistant called her 30 days later to set up a lunch meeting at one of the nicest restaurants in town, she was floored. Seven years later, Natalie continues to meet with that mentor for lunch twice a year. Their mentoring relationship has flourished and has been fully rewarding.

Healthcare management is a competitive field, so take the initiative to get creative with your approach to stand out from the crowd. So what, if you get more "no" than "yes," more doubters than believers? Take that calculated risk. But whatever strategic move you make, ensure that it is always professional, always appropriate, and never too over the top that you're attracting the wrong kind of attention.

STRENGTHENING YOUR WORK ETHIC

A strong work ethic shares the same DNA with strong character. That is, if your work ethic is superb, you take ownership of your performance and results, you care about the quality of your work, you're a team player but capable of working independently, you're honest about your knowledge and skills, and you do more than what the assignment or project requires. In other words, you have integrity that enables others to trust you as well as deem you responsible and credible.

A commitment to strengthening your work ethic requires both self-discipline and mental discipline. We're not going to discuss the intricacies of mental discipline here, but suffice it to say that if self-discipline is *how hard* you work, then mental discipline is *how well* you work. When you're mentally disciplined, you are in control of how you think about and respond to situations and you can choose to be positive rather than negative.

Some of the small acts you could do include the following:

1. *Change your attitude.* You may be the hardest worker around, but if you're grumpy, negative, or disengaged, you may not find willing volunteers or helpers for your projects. No one wants to work with an unhappy person or someone with a chip on her shoulders. Not only is attitude contagious, but it can also hamper your career.

2. *Manage your time.* If you know you tend to procrastinate or get distracted easily, start your projects early and ask for an extension as soon as necessary. Not meeting your deadlines is understandable if it happens only sometimes. But if it happens all the time, then it will affect not only the types of projects you are assigned but also your professional reputation. The worst thing you can do is use excuses or rationalize why you are late. Own up to your mistake and apologize.

3. *Be strategic.* See the next section.

STRATEGIC COMMITMENT, NOT SACRIFICE

When you commit to developing your career, you may not realize what it all entails until you're neck-deep into it. For example, you may know that studying for the ACHE board certification exam would take a lot of time, but you may not know that it could take 10 to 15 hours a week. That's a huge chunk of time away from your loved ones, your hobbies, and anything else that matters to you. Of course, as we've said over and over again, you have a choice: Put in the hard work and enjoy the long-term benefits, or opt out and enjoy the short-term relief but suffer the long-term consequences.

There is no shortcut to personal and professional growth. No quick fixes. No magic wand. But there is such a thing as changing your mind-set so that you don't view the work involved as a painstaking sacrifice but rather as a conscious strategic commitment. Take Laurie's story, for example.

As a young professional, Laurie left a healthcare executive job to launch her own consulting practice. She wanted the time flexibility that the business afforded her so that she could be present for her husband and young children and still continue to fulfill her professional aspirations as an industry leader and entrepreneur. Although, technically, she gave things up—like a guaranteed paycheck, a collegial team environment, daily access to colleagues and superiors, and the support and resources of an established organization—she never saw those losses or her decision as a sacrifice. Instead, she deemed the move as a strategic choice or commitment.

Laurie went on to pursue board certification from both ACHE and ACMPE (American College of Medical Practice Executives), giving up months' worth of time to study for board exams and write case studies and an academic paper. Her strategic commitment paid off. She earned the certifications, a distinction that fewer than 15 percent of her contemporaries in the industry possess.

What if you, too, started looking at decisions in your life as strategic commitments (gains) rather than sacrifices (losses)? Start small.

Say you commit to growing your network but you don't have time to attend networking events. You don't have to sacrifice a Saturday or Sunday or even a weeknight to do that, you could just go during lunch. Instead of dining with your regular lunch group every day, pick a day or two during the week to have lunch with those you want to network with. This way, you not only keep your set of work friends but you also gain new associates.

Changing your mind-set, changing your attitude, making conscious or strategic decisions, turning negatives into positives—whatever you want to call it, it works. It's a part of the framework of commitment and self-discipline. Go ahead and give it a try!

Rookie Mistakes

Coasting

It's easy to coast through a job when you're just starting out. No one is expecting you to shoot straight to the C-suite. No one is pressuring you to go back to school to update your skills. No one is giving you complicated or high-traffic departments to run on your own. And that's precisely why you shouldn't be complacent. You have to take control of your career early and always. If you don't, you could remain under the radar. Commit to advancing your career, and do the difficult work necessary to prove that commitment.

Being Strategic, Not Tactical

Eric was an administrative fellow in a health system. One day, he volunteered to take and then distribute the minutes for senior management meetings—meetings he had no reason to be in. His mentor, the president, agreed. Eric found the task tedious and unglamorous . . .

Now let's stop here for a pop quiz: Did Eric make a mistake? Yes, no, maybe? Why? This is not an open-book quiz, so don't look ahead to the rest of the story.

. . . but it afforded him unparalleled access to the inner workings of the system and allowed him to build stronger relationships with key executives. The experience was incredibly valuable to Eric's career development.

What was your answer? Did you guess how the story ended? How?

Healthcare is replete with clever, true stories like this. This one demonstrates the value of being strategic rather than

→

tactical. When you're tactical, you think in terms of the here and now (the short term). When you're strategic, you think of the far and away (the long term). The problem with being tactical is that it doesn't allow you a view of the big picture. And if you fail to see the big picture, you miss out on unique and strategic opportunities that offer great rewards. Change your mind-set and start to make conscious, strategic moves. Then, create and share your own success story.

Staying Isolated

When you land your first healthcare job, learn the ropes of your new position, and get comfortable with the idea of busy professionals of all types consulting and commiserating with you, you may start to think that there's no more need to try, that you have found the tribe you belong with for the rest of your career, and that networking is now a thing of the past. But you'd be wrong. It's good to make connections with people at work, but it's also worthwhile to expand your reach to those outside of your immediate circle. After all, you might want to change careers, organizations, or industries later. The more relationships you build now, the greater the likelihood that those people will still be there to support you later.

Remember These

- Conscious commitment is the voluntary, mindful dedication to something.
- Self-discipline involves the ability to be more discerning about your choices and to remove yourself from tempting situations that might be enjoyable today but could hurt you in the future. →

- Self-disciplined people don't use adversity, setbacks, or discomfort as an excuse. They persevere, despite their strong impulse to quit, postpone, or forget about the activity they committed to.

- Small, disciplined acts when practiced consistently turn into habits or automatic responses. In turn, the small things add up and result in huge changes in how you enter into a commitment and how you fulfill that commitment.

- Gaining benefits shouldn't be the only reason you are forging a connection with someone.

- To be highly productive and highly successful in your line of work, you have to do what's necessary. And often what's necessary is difficult and frustrating and demanding.

- Self-discipline is *how hard* you work, while mental discipline is *how well* you work. When you're mentally disciplined, you are in control of how you think about and respond to situations and you can choose to be positive rather than negative.

- There is no shortcut to personal and professional growth. No quick fixes. No magic wand. But there is such a thing as changing your mind-set so that you don't view the work involved as a painstaking sacrifice but rather as a conscious strategic commitment.

REFERENCES

Olson, J. 2011. *The Slight Edge: Turning Simple Disciplines Into Massive Success,* Revised Edition. Lake Dallas, TX: Success Books.

Strom, D. 2013. "What Recruiters Look for in a 6-Second Resume Scan." Posted June 9. http://news.dice.com/2013/01/09/what-recruiter-look-for-in-a-6-second-resume-scan/

Szalavitz, M. 2013. "Self-Disciplined People Are Happier (and Not as Deprived as You Think)." *Time*. Posted June 24. http://healthland.time.com/2013/06/24 /self-disciplined-people-are-happier-and-not-as-deprived-as-you-think/.

ADDITIONAL RESOURCE

Hoffmann, W., M. Luhmann, R. R. Fisher, K. D. Vohs, and R. F. Baumeister. "Yes, But Are They Happy? Effects of Trait Self-Control on Affecting Well-Being and Life Satisfaction." *Journal of Personality* 82 (4): 265–77.

PART II

Building and Maintaining a Forward-Moving Career

IN PART I, we covered the foundational concepts and approaches for developing you—the way you conduct yourself, interact with and influence others, and do your work—so that you can stand head and shoulders above the rest. In Part II, we pull from these basics and expand our discussion to include strategies and tactics that help you build and grow a career in the competitive and challenging field of healthcare management.

Specifically, we address why it's important to curate (read: be cautious about) what you share on social media and why it's advisable to match your online brand to your authentic offline persona. We also talk about understanding what you're doing (performance), how you're doing it (style), and how that style could help or hamper both. Plus, we explain the principle of servant leadership, a model focused on the others instead of the self; the inevitability of failures; the art of forming and nurturing relationships (aka networking); and the importance of finding and becoming a mentor.

Our goal in these chapters is to emphasize that career building and maintenance is not a solitary, stable pursuit but rather an activity that relies on other people and that involves many ups and downs. Don't want to police your behavior, take risks, reach out to others, try new things, fail every once in a while, and serve your stakeholders? Then expect to be stuck, to find yourself in the same spot year after year while your peers move on and up. When you read the Note to My 25-Year-Old Self features scattered throughout this book, you'll see that our recommendations are echoed by the same people who have led and still are leading the field today.

CHAPTER 5

Cultivate Your Personal Brand

*"Your brand is what people say about you
when you're not in the room."*

Jeff Bezos, Founder, Amazon.com

Reading Points

- Finding the True You

- Curating Your Online Posts

- Maintaining Professional Decorum

- Networking on Social Media

NAME A BRAND, any brand. Did you name your favorites? Did you name yourself? Are you aware that you are a brand as well?

A personal brand is all about what an individual represents and how that image is perceived. Specifically, your brand includes your name, gender, occupation, character, education and training, personal and professional style (including leadership style; see Chapter 6), skills and talents, accomplishments, associations, and reputation. If you're on social media, your brand is represented by your posts; photos; status updates; comments or responses; things you "like," favorited, or upvoted; tags; links shared or forwarded; and following and follower lists. These are the details people associate with your brand—both offline (or "in real life") and online. Like consumer brands, your personal brand elicits conscious and subconscious reactions from anyone who meets, talks to, or hears about you. If these people were playing a word-association game, what do you think they'd say when your name comes up?

Keep your offline and online personas consistent with each other. That is, be aware of the discrepancy between who you are in real life and who you seem to be on the computer screen. Contradictions between the two often send the message that you're not living your authentic self. For example, if friends, family, coworkers, and bosses know you as a caring, intelligent individual, they will be shocked and dismayed if you tweeted something that bullies or shames anyone—whether in a personal or professional context. Don't confuse and surprise your audience, as they have the power to tarnish your brand—that is, if your own behavior doesn't tarnish it first.

In this age of do-it-yourself everything, the Web seems to have become the number-one tool for finding information about a person. Even if you're not an active Web user, you still have an online presence. What will a simple Google search of your name reveal about your brand? Will it turn up your social media accounts? Awards and achievements? Embarrassing posts or selfies? Good or bad, the answers are the reason you should continually cultivate your personal brand. The better you are offline, the better you'll look online.

This chapter offers the dos and don'ts of cultivating your brand. As usual, we present examples, recommendations, and tips.

FINDING THE TRUE YOU

Self-awareness, the result of self-reflection, is the first multilayered step to cultivating your brand (see Chapter 1). When you have a strong grasp of who you are, you can better manage and improve your interactions and relationships, your self-development needs, other's expectations and reactions to you, your influence on others, and so on. Equally important is that you become more authentic, aware of your abilities and accomplishments but at the same time humbled by your own limitations and weaknesses and by your "work-in-progress" status. This kind of authenticity is important to your brand because it makes you relatable.

Although we've addressed self-awareness strategies extensively in Chapter 1, we review some small-act tips here:

- *Step outside yourself.* How do you see yourself? How do you think others see you? What types of people do you attract and attract you, and why? Would you hire or fire someone like you, and why? Do your activities and behavior in and out of work embarrass or inspire others? Do you edit parts of yourself or your experiences in discussions or conversations, and why or why not? What things about you are you proud to tell others, and which would you rather keep to yourself? Have others criticized you in the past, and what did you do with that information? What one word would your coworkers or bosses use to describe you? These questions will trigger other probing questions. Answer them honestly; you don't have to report your findings to anyone, but you do have to act on them.

- *Ask a friend, family member, coworker, or mentor to be honest about you.* Give them permission to be as candid as possible, and reassure them that their opinions would not affect your relationship (although they could hurt your feelings). Try not to be defensive about the details they bring up; they are not attacking you but giving you much needed feedback. And that feedback could range from how you communicate verbally, in writing, and with your body (e.g., do you speak clearly? are your e-mails, papers, tweets, reports, and texts riddled with typos and/or slang? do you look people in the eyes? is your handshake firm?) to how you conduct yourself professionally (e.g., do you show up late to meetings? do you pay attention or listen without distractions? is your attire business appropriate? are you reliable and do you take responsibility for your mistakes?) to what attitudes you typically display (e.g., are you an optimist or a pessimist? do you welcome or avoid change? are you snarky and sarcastic or compassionate and sensitive?).

- *Make a list of what makes you uniquely you.* This includes your beliefs, likes and dislikes, talents, skills, character traits, behavioral tendencies, achievements and failures, types of people you associate with, personal and professional goals, activities or causes you participate in, and any other components that define who you are.

- *Review your online and offline activities.* Your social network profiles, comments on various sites, blog posts, tweets, posted pictures and videos, and all other activities on the Web don't exist in a vacuum. The same goes for offline activities. Knowing what you spend your time on is a good step to understanding the *you* brand.

Revisit these small acts periodically. Invest time quarterly or annually to take stock of your growth. Be honest. Be intentional. And remember that what gets measured, gets managed.

One caveat: Although you should embrace (and celebrate) your authentic self, you must consider how it affects those around you. Be careful about (or even change) the aspects of you that could potentially cause more harm than good to your brand, especially when displayed online, where it's hard to retract what you say and do.

CURATING YOUR ONLINE POSTS

In the years before Facebook and Twitter (gasp!), defining your personal brand meant how you conducted yourself at networking events and what catchphrase was written on your business card. If you wanted your brand to take a slightly different direction or if you made a mistake, no problem! All you had to do was change your strategy or behavior going forward, and all was well. That's not as true today because most of us now work and play on the Web, where all our personal and professional actions and decisions can be viewed with a quick search—even if we don't use our real name.

If you're a 24-year-old MHA graduate, for example, and you've been on Facebook since you were 15, guess what? Your status updates from nine years ago—when you were still in high school—are still just as much a part of your personal brand as your Facebook activities today. Same goes for old photos, old videos, and old comments you shared online. Scary, but true.

Our point is not to scare you, though. We're here to remind you that what is posted today will be around for a long time—most likely permanently. Juvenile activities could harm your brand and thus your chances for a huge promotion, an interview for a dream job, or any other once-in-a-lifetime opportunity. It's no secret anymore that employers put on their sleuthing caps and search the Web for any (negative and positive) information on a prospective or current employee.

Although you can't do anything about the past, you can control what you do today. Err on the side of caution and agonize too much, rather than too little, over a post than to just let everything fly without considering the consequences or the blow to your brand. Avoid such consequences with these three basic but self-disciplined steps:

1. *Review your privacy settings.* You can adjust how much of your social media profiles that your family members,

friends, colleagues, and the general public can see or access. But remember this: Even with the most conservative or restrictive privacy settings, that inappropriate photo or post you or someone else uploaded can still find its way into the hands of employers and those who can make your shame viral. You could pay huge amounts of money for a reputation management company to sweep the Web of all the negative images and posts related to you, but this effort may not be enough.

2. *Filter yourself.* As we mention over and over again, self-awareness—along with self-discipline—is critical. The more aware you are of how others perceive you (and the implications of those perceptions), the more likely you will think before posting. For each status update, comment, tweet, or photo upload, ask yourself this: Does this really align with the professional image I want to project? Or more simply, will I regret this? When in doubt, leave it out.

3. *Bite your tongue.* Never, ever speak ill of your job, colleagues, and employers. Online, everything and everyone should be regarded as great. Your job is a dream. Your colleagues are fantastic. Your boss is the best ever. Your workplace can't be beat. These may not be true in reality, but online is not the place for you to air out your dirty laundry. We're not suggesting that you lie, but we're arguing that you should not burn bridges or disregard people's feelings. If you will not say negative and hurtful words to anyone to their face or within their earshot, then you must not type disparaging comments about anyone online. The two are essentially the same thing. If you must (for some reason) include the people and the place that employ you in your conversation, don't complain. No matter how cryptic, witty, or disguised your criticism is, it can be identified and can get back to those you're

targeting. Depending on your company's social media policy, you may be handed a box of your belongings and escorted out of the building the next time you show up to work.

No one is too big or too valuable to be fired. Even owners, board chairs, and CEOs can and have fallen into this trap. So be careful what you say out there!

MAINTAINING PROFESSIONAL DECORUM

Wear professional business attire, be well groomed, and maintain good personal hygiene. Modulate your voice, enunciate, articulate, and don't use words you don't fully understand. Don't slouch, keep your chin up, firmly shake hands (don't crush or jerk), and look people in the eye. Show confidence, humility, respect, and gratitude. Do all of this when you first meet people, during official work functions, and for job interviews. We know we sound like a drill sergeant, but this is an important message that we cannot deliver less directly. Professional decorum elevates the *you* brand; no one will dispute that. And as we say in our sessions, carry yourself *as if* you are already filling the job of your dreams.

Looks Matter

Let's talk about your appearance—specifically, the way you dress and the way you present to others. In the modern, more sensitive world we live in, it's almost taboo to talk about judging people based on looks. But let's be realistic: It happens, even if we don't intend for it to happen.

The blind-audition portion of the popular TV show *The Voice* gives aspiring singers a chance to showcase their abilities to a panel of superstar judges whose backs are turned so that they cannot see the performers. The contestants focus on singing and nothing else because they know they are only going to be judged on their voice, not their appearance. Unfortunately, the rest of society does not work like *The Voice*.

People do judge you for how you look, and the sooner you accept that, the better off you'll be. Professionals have long held that it takes only a few minutes to make a first impression on someone, while others argue that we only get about 30 seconds. Author Malcolm Gladwell (2007) claims that it's even faster—one to two seconds maximum. You have only those quick seconds to make as strong a first impression as possible and to judge or make up your mind about those who are standing in front of you.

Again, this comes back to self-awareness. Look in that mirror, and be honest about what message you are sending with your appearance. Better yet, ask a friend for their frank assessment. You might love your personal style (e.g., trendy clothes and accessories, colorful hair, visible piercings and tattoos), but consider how that style translates in a professional, formal environment. What message is it sending to a job recruiter or a future boss, and how is it tainting their perception of you? They don't yet know that, beneath the style (which might intimidate some people), there is an incredibly smart, creative, capable, and hardworking you. It's their loss, right? Wrong. It's your lost opportunity—and preventable loss at that.

Every work environment or culture operates by a set of rules, including the dress code. When you are trying to fit in or dress appropriately, you have to match your appearance with the appearance of everyone else in the organization. For example, if everyone (including the CEO) at your small, rural community hospital wears khakis, cotton shirts, and tennis shoes, you have to dress in the same way. How will you relate to them if you show up in a pinstriped suit and designer loafers every day? The opposite is also true. If your board members always wear formal professional attire (i.e., suit and tie for men; dress suit or pantsuit for women), then you do the same on the day you're meeting with or presenting to them—even if the outfit is not what you wear to work on a daily basis. If you're meeting with the property maintenance team for a once-a-year, all-day logistics strategy session for the organization's big events of the year, show up in jeans and a t-shirt branded with the hospital logo—just like the team members wear all the time. Dressing according to the accepted style of a work group or the culture helps you gain instant acceptance and earn some of your coworkers' trust, whether or not they realize that is what's happening.

For example, Anna worked in a hospital's IT department. She was one of a handful of women who worked among a throng of male computer programmers. It was a jeans-only environment, so for the first few days on the job, she showed up in skinny jeans and high heels. She looked like a professional knockout. The programmers, on the other hand, struggled to tuck in their unironed shirts or to find jeans that didn't end three inches above the top of their shoes. Needless to say, they were intimidated by her. Anna realized this soon enough, though. When she returned to work wearing relaxed-fit jeans and flats, she found that her ability to communicate effectively with the programmers magically and suddenly improved.

The point of all this is that when it comes to managing your personal self (personality and style included) and your professional self (leadership style included), it takes a fine balance. Work is not always the appropriate place to express your true personality, especially if you are a newcomer. You often have to conform your personality (in this case, your appearance) to the environment, not the other way around. But that is not to say that your personality—which is a strong part of your personal brand and the very first piece of that brand exposed to the people around you—should be locked out of the workplace. How much or how little of your personality to take with you on a regular basis is up to you. But be aware that, in the professional setting, you must make sure your personal brand is sending the message that you want to convey. The same is expected of you on social media.

NETWORKING ON SOCIAL MEDIA

With social media, there has never been an easier time than today to build your personal brand. Now instead of only being able to network at in-person gatherings—such as your health administration program's sponsored events or a healthcare association's annual conference (like the ACHE Congress)—you can also network online. And you can do it efficiently and effectively. Just like networking in person, networking online isn't about meeting someone and immediately asking for the "sale." It's about getting to know people and building relationships—relationships that can provide mutual benefits for months and years down the road.

How to get started? Establish an account on LinkedIn and Twitter, for example. Scan or search for thought leaders on your topics of interest. Who are the favorite authors, speakers, or bloggers in your industry or other related fields? Who are prominent executives from your organization, your community, and your profession? Follow them, as well as associations, publications, or organizations whose work relates to your work, your interests, or your aspirations. On Twitter, you may search using hashtags, to find information and contributors by topic (e.g., #leadership, #innovation, #patientsafety) or using the monikers promoted by specific conferences or events (e.g., #ACHE2015).

The number-one mistake professionals make online is failing to remember that interacting and networking on the Web requires the same respect and the same decorum as interacting and networking face to face. The second biggest mistake? Forgetting that online, everything is visible and everything is permanent, as we've said earlier. But if you conduct yourself *as if*, you should be fine.

In this section, we're not going to list the various social media sites out there and how they can help you network. Because the Web and technology are ever advancing, these specific sites and applications change quickly. Do keep tabs on online networking trends throughout your career. For now, Twitter, Facebook, and

LinkedIn are the most popular among professionals. Our recommendation is to use Facebook for personal, LinkedIn for professional, and Twitter for a blend of the two.

Dedicating each site to a specific use is a good way to remain consistent with your message in each platform. For example, if you regularly share healthcare-related news, MHA class information, and other helpful industry or career resources on LinkedIn, then your networks or connections know that you are on the site for professional or business purposes. Don't suddenly switch to discussing the best chili recipes—save that for Facebook! If you are using Twitter for both personal and professional purposes, make sure that you maintain professional decorum, even though you may not always be tweeting about work. Keep it clean (including being selective about whom you follow and which retweets you send under your name), as you are representing the *you* brand to all your followers.

When networking online, you must be self-aware, smart, and authentic. You must also be cautious. Be cognizant of the fact that you are not just the main face of your personal brand but also an indirect representative of your current organization—even if you aren't the organization's official spokesperson, publicist, or account/profile administrator. If the organization is listed on your resumé, bio, or CV as your employer, then your words and actions reflect upon that company. Take that responsibility seriously.

We saved the best for last: Offline and online, the more defined your personal brand, the more value it holds. As you progress in your career and if you continue to improve yourself and cultivate your brand, you won't need to search endlessly for greater roles and new opportunities. Those things will come to you. Your brand will speak for itself, your robust network will support you, and you will get offers. For now, you have work to do.

Rookie Mistakes

Tweeting Like No One's Watching

Several years ago, during an industry conference, Laurie stumbled on a tweet by another attendee. The tweet was a pleasant, professionally composed compliment to the organization that put together the conference. Laurie was quite impressed with the message, so she decided to click on the name of the attendee to find out more. He turned out to be a new MHA graduate looking for his first job in healthcare. And then Laurie scrolled down to read his other tweets, and that was when she wished she hadn't. His past tweets (some as recent as two days before the conference) were full of foul language, rude and arrogant remarks, and other not-safe-for-work musings. And they were all public, all out there for the world to see. Laurie doesn't know what became of him; all she knows is that she could never endorse, hire, or network with someone as self-*un*aware as he was.

Dressing for the Nightclub

Natalie once interviewed for a very competitive job. All the candidates were highly accomplished. One in particular (let's call him Joe) had qualifications that mirrored those of Natalie. He was a sprint runner in college, just like her. And he even taught middle school, just as she did. On interview day, Joe wore a nice suit—and a colorful printed shirt with no tie. In fact, his shirt was open to reveal an undershirt. His hair could use a comb, and his shoes could be a lot less pointy. Frankly, he looked like he just got home from the club.

After a long day of interviews, Natalie got the job.

→

To be fair, Joe didn't land the job *not just* because of what he looked like. But his appearance certainly didn't win him points. Perhaps had he shown up in professional attire, the interviewees might have viewed him as a more serious contender and might not have been too quick to eliminate him from the tight competition. The small details of his appearance—especially the opened, printed shirt—were not just distracting but also sent a clear message that his head was not in the game that day and that he was not ready for the next level.

Remember These

- The better you are offline, the better you'll look online.
- Your personal brand elicits conscious and subconscious reactions from anyone who meets, talks to, or hears about you.
- Conduct yourself *as if* you're already filling the job of your dreams.
- Keep your offline and online personas consistent with each other.
- When you are authentic, you're aware of your abilities and accomplishments but at the same time humbled by your own limitations and weaknesses and by your "work-in-progress" status. This kind of authenticity is important to your brand because it makes you relatable.
- Err on the side of caution and agonize too much, rather than too little, over an online post than to just let everything fly without considering the consequences. When in doubt, don't.

→

- You have only a few seconds to make as strong a first impression as possible and to judge or make up your mind about those who are standing in front of you.

- How much or how little of your personality to take with you on a regular basis is up to you. But be aware that, in the professional setting, you must make sure your personal brand is sending the message that you want to convey. The same is expected of you on social media.

- Just like networking in person, networking online isn't about meeting someone and immediately asking for the "sale." It's about getting to know people and building relationships—relationships that can provide mutual benefits for months and years down the road.

REFERENCE

Gladwell, M. 2007. *Blink: The Power of Thinking Without Thinking.* New York: Back Bay Books.

CHAPTER 6

Identify and Develop Your Leadership Style

"Our emerging workforce is not interested in
command-and-control leadership.
They don't want to do things because I said so;
they want to do things because they want to do them."

—*Irene Rosenfeld, CEO, Mondelēz International*

Reading Points

- Follow
- Learn from Mistakes
- Show You Care
- Pay Attention to Culture
- Take Ownership
- Be Cognizant of the Company You Keep
- Build on Your Inherent Strengths and Talents

DON'T WAIT UNTIL you're a CEO, director, vice president, or some other high-level executive to start adopting approaches that enhance your leadership style and performance. By then, it will be

95

too late. You'll have already etched your personal brand in people's minds that follows you from one organization to the next. And people's long-held perceptions are the hardest to convert. So start now when you've just entered the healthcare door. You don't have to be a formal leader to act like a leader.

This chapter highlights some good practices that any professional at any level can follow to boost interaction, work performance, influence, and effect on others. We present them here in no particular order because, at the end of the day, only you can decide which approach should take precedence over another.

FOLLOW

Followers get a bad rap in our individualistic society. Parents scold their children with the classic don't-be-a-follower line "If all your friends jumped off a bridge, would you jump, too?!" Adults label those who conform as "sheeple." Hanger-on, peon, yes-man, minion, and so many other unflattering terms are indiscriminately used to describe a person who proudly supports or serves another. Hollywood perpetuates the image of followers as boring and traditional while nonfollowers as romantic and modern.

But perception often skews the truth. And the truth is not everyone can be a leader. And the other truth is being a follower is not the weak-willed obedience to a mindless activity, person, viewpoint, or rule that society wants us to believe it is—at least not in the workplace. Instead, being a follower is an act of active participation, especially if you're working for a participative leader. That is, if you choose to follow deliberately (not out of impulse, thrill, or blind faith), you typically have

- a reason, a motivation, or an agenda;
- trust or confidence in the person (she's proven she knows what she's doing) or in the idea (everything will work out as planned);

- a desire to contribute something (including moral support) that helps the person or activity to function or move forward;
- team or group orientation (you believe you can accomplish more or achieve better results with others than on your own); and
- critical thinking skills that allow you to identify the pros and cons of what you're getting into.

Robert Kelley (1992), one of the first academics to examine the concept of followership in the workplace, estimated that followers "actually contribute more than 80 percent to the success of any project, any organization, while leaders at best contribute only 20 percent." Think about that. This means two things: (1) followers carry out the vision, strategies, and plans leaders have crafted, and (2) leaders use followers' feedback, recommendations, perspectives, opinions, observations, and so on to spark or polish their own ideas.

We think that what leaders (regardless of style) want, though, are more than just warm-bodied followers. They want *good* followers. And by that we mean those who not only possess the requisite competency, work ethic, and interpersonal skills but who also

- are honest, trustworthy, credible, and respectful;
- don't take or give abuse;
- have problem-solving and creative skills;
- take full responsibility for their mistakes and take the initiative to correct them;
- are eager to learn and teach others;
- can and want to work with other people; and
- are not afraid of constructive feedback.

Followers of this caliber are self-starters and self-managers. They are role models for the rest of the team and may be called upon to run a meeting, monitor an initiative, or do something high level in the absence of the leader.

One of the often-repeated maxims of management is that leaders, in order to be good leaders, must first learn to be good followers. Why? Because followership requires humility, listening more than talking, giving more than taking, learning more than teaching, and teaching more than dictating. Leadership should require the same. Following doesn't make a leader less decisive or less in control—but more secure in knowing that reliable and capable followers "got his back," so to speak, and have the organization's best interest at heart.

Incorporate followership into your style and then watch yourself improve, little by little, at being a leader.

LEARN FROM MISTAKES

Errors, missteps, unfortunate circumstances, and bumps in the road are inevitable. They will happen during your career—several times. And *when* (never *if*) they do, they will hurt and cause you to become discouraged, wrestle with your identity, and lose your self-confidence. It's tempting to sulk, hide, make excuses, or blame someone else. But none of these reactions leads you to a workable solution. So brush off these negative thoughts and keep on truckin'! Don't let the mistakes damage you (your brand or your team) and make you ineffective. Instead, rise above them and listen to what they're telling you.

Mistakes typically sound the alarm on things that are being ignored, that need fixing or correcting, or that operate under false assumptions. Identify and then address those issues. Be honest with yourself. Ask for feedback, and be receptive to criticisms. Consult with your support system or network (including your mentor). Apologize or express your regret.

If learning from your own mistakes is good, learning from the mistakes of others is even better. Your mentor, coworkers, boss,

CEO and other executives in your organization, and associates in your network are a fantastic source in this regard. Ask them (if you've already established a rapport) what their most embarrassing mistake has been so far and what they learned from it. Observe, if you can, how they handle mistakes. You won't know all the details, but you'll have a general idea of the what, the how, and the why. Add all of this to your understanding and experience. You never know, one day you could apply these second-hand lessons to your own challenges.

SHOW YOU CARE

Allow others to see that you care. Now, don't do a few kind things every once in a while just to show off to people that you're "caring." People—from the CEO to the receptionist—will see right through you! Be authentic. Show others that your healthcare career is not just a job but a true calling, a passion. Show others that you're there to serve.

So how should you show (not just say) that you care?

1. *Treat everyone with respect and kindness*—every day and in whatever mood you're in and despite whatever pressures you're facing. Don't do it to be magnanimous or to impress an audience. Do it because you're a decent human being.

2. *Learn and fully participate in the culture.* "When in Rome, do as the Romans do," as the old adage goes. For you, it means embracing the unofficial and staff-driven rules, traditions, and mores of your department and the organization. Don't criticize or make fun of the culture, and if you find something inappropriate or uncomfortable about it, let it go or talk to your boss. If you can't participate, do so without making a fuss.

3. *Do the right thing.* This may be easier said than done because in healthcare it isn't always easy to tell the "good" from the "bad" side, especially during a conflict. But do weigh both sides or the pros and cons of each. Lean on your convictions. Follow policies. Seek advice from others in the organization. Communicate with the parties involved. Being thoughtful about how you approach a problem sends a message that you are doing your best to make things right.

4. *Show up—and be prepared and on time.* When you show up ready, things get done. And when things get done, people see that you are there to work as hard as they do, that you care about their time and don't want to waste it, and that you're trying hard to do your part.

5. *Offer help and moral support.* This is such a small gesture that means a lot. It builds people's morale, lets them know they are not alone, and relieves some of their stress.

Other ways you can show you care include being sympathetic and empathetic, acknowledging people's contributions and accomplishments, joining in on the fun (whether it's a potluck or a small birthday party or a company picnic), and not being a pushover or not making the tough but appropriate and fair call. (It's not caring if you are allowing people to take advantage of your kindness.)

Having a caring and authentic leadership style encourages those around you to lower their defensiveness and to up their game to match yours. Over time, your efforts to show you care compound and your influence on others grows.

PAY ATTENTION TO CULTURE

The way we do things around here. That's the most direct way of defining organizational culture, which exists in every company and even in departments. It could be as eccentric as an older gentleman standing in the lobby to greet passersby and urge them to play the piano sitting a few feet away. Or as amazing as an ongoing competition over which nurses' station can drink the most office coffee every month. Or as endearing as an annual clown parade thrown by a children's hospital for its patients and their parents but attended by the entire community.

When you become part of a culture, don't be just a spectator, laughing and clapping on the sidelines. You gotta get in it! Play the piano even if you don't know how. Join the nurses for a cup o' joe. Offer to throw out candy during the parade.

When Natalie took her first CEO position at a small critical access hospital in Colorado, she wanted to immerse herself in the community's culture immediately. She was set on proving that she was happy to be there and was eager to get to know the people. So what did she do? Within the first six months, she had enrolled in night school and earned an EMT certificate to serve the town's voluntary ambulance department, graduated from square dancing lessons, gone combining for corn with the chairman of the hospital's board of directors, learned to shoot clay pigeons, and joined the local gun club. She left all of her dark business suits in her closet and embraced the adventure.

Natalie took the same approach in the hospital. Through close observation, she discovered that the cook, who had worked there for decades, was one of the most beloved employees. Everyone valued and respected her opinion. As such, she represented the informal leaders in an organization. Natalie knew that if she wanted to understand the culture, she could question the cook and learn.

Informal leaders are a big deal because they are very influential on other staff. Getting to know them is like getting a taste or a whiff of what's cooking in the organization, so to speak. That is to say, these informal leaders know or represent how the rest of the employees think, how they may react to a change initiative, what they may find acceptable and nonnegotiable, and what they may support or push back against.

If your leadership style is strategic, make a habit of being involved in the culture, including the subcultures. Identify how the leader's style makes or breaks a culture and inspires the best performance.

TAKE OWNERSHIP

Cerner Corporation, an electronic medical record software company based in Kansas City, Missouri, teaches every new employee the company principle called "kill the snake" (Sorensen 2014). No, they're not reptile haters. The phrase means if you see a problem, fix it. Doesn't matter whose problem. Doesn't matter who caused it. You spotted it, you take care of it. Period. What Cerner warns its employees never to do is to see a snake and then walk away from it as if it didn't even rear its ugly head. That snake will one day come back and bite everyone.

This philosophy perfectly exemplifies what taking ownership is all about. It's not about taking the fall for someone else; it's about looking out for the interest of the whole group, not just your own, so that no one takes a tumble—but if that happens, that person is not going to fall alone. In other words, taking ownership is a *we* thing, not an *I* thing.

When you take ownership of a project, for example, you are fully engaged. You care that everyone involved is doing their part according to the time line, the objectives, the expected quality, and so on. If they are not, then you offer help for the sake of moving the project forward. If the project turns out to be unsatisfactory, you share the blame and the responsibility for fixing the issue—even though you did your part correctly. If the project turns out well, you congratulate everyone for a job well done and share the credit.

While you work, do you practice "kill the snake"? If not, how do you handle that snake when it reappears? Are you having to do a lot of work-arounds or engage in redundancies because of it? How can you adjust your style so that you can take more ownership and do your job more efficiently?

BE COGNIZANT OF THE COMPANY YOU KEEP

Think about your immediate family, then your extended family. Think about your significant other, close friends, then your acquaintances. Think about your mentors and advisors. Think about your coworkers, including your boss and everyone else you work with. Think about your social media network or followers. All these people are in your sphere of influence—the people you have influence over and who have influence over you. These people shape who you are personally and professionally and are part of the reasons you do what you do.

Now, answer these questions:

- Who pushes you to be a better person?
- Who encourages you in all your pursuits, including personal and professional development?
- Who gave you the idea to go into healthcare management?
- Who are your biggest influencers?
- Who is just like you—same profession, same ambition, same short-term and long-term goals, same attitude, and so on?
- Who helps you set goals and change habits?
- Who is most and least responsive to you—either online or offline?
- Who is your cheerleader?
- Who is your rock?
- Who can you always turn to for help, to talk to, or confide in?
- Who is your biggest critic (outside of you)? Naysayer? Rival?
- Who discourages or makes fun of your personal and professional efforts?
- Whose life, career path, future goals, general beliefs used to mimic yours but are now opposite from yours?

- Do you consider the people who surround you a negative or a positive force in your life?
- Who affects you positively or negatively? In what way?
- Do you like hanging out with them? If not, why not?
- Are you outgrowing some of your friends? Are they outgrowing you? Do you still share something in common with them? Why not?
- Whom haven't you seen or talked to in at least one year?
- Whom do you need or want to cut ties from?

Asking yourself these questions reveal who in your sphere of influence affects you the most and the least and what effect they have on you. Negative influencers can push you off course and leave you stranded, while positive influencers will pull you in the right direction. By taking this inventory occasionally, you can make a decision to reduce or increase the time you spend with certain people. You may find you've outgrown some people or that your views and priorities are no longer in sync with theirs. (Exhibit 6.1 discusses two theories of influence.)

The company you keep has the power to strengthen or weaken your performance. If your sphere of influence is supportive and enthusiastic about your efforts to grow personally and

---

Exhibit 6.1 The Average Five and The Sixth Man Theories

Motivational speaker Jim Rohn theorizes that "you are the average of the five people closest to you." That means almost everything an adult is—character, behavior, abilities, fears, occupation or ambition, accomplishments, failures, likes and dislikes, and so on—is shaped or influenced by the people she spends the most time with. And she, in turn, influences someone else's life, and on it goes. As a result, each of us has beliefs and interests that mirror those of our friends, family members, and significant others.

For example, if you're a fitness freak, your best friend is, too. If you're religious or political or into social activism, one or both of your parents may

(continued)

have passed that value to you. And if you're a spendthrift or extravagant, you learned that behavior from someone close to you now or in the past.

The lesson here is simple: Be mindful and deliberate about selecting the people you associate with. Befriend those whose interests are similar or complementary to yours or from whom you can learn a lot. Let go of those whose presence or influence is negative.

Apply this theory to yourself. Does it work for you?

Now let's extend this concept to what we'll call "The Sixth Man" (patterned after the Texas A&M football program's Twelfth Man notion of its fans being the twelfth member of the 11-man team on the field). The sixth man doesn't have to be a man or even a person. It's a force that represents the thing (not a person) that causes you to do what you do. It could be your spirit, free will, words of wisdom or words of doubt, a hole inside you that needs to be filled, that thing that keeps you up at night, a goal or dream, a hobby, and so on. Let's give you an example.

Many years ago, we both had the privilege of meeting the brilliant Ben Carson, the now-retired pediatric neurosurgeon. He grew up dirt poor in Detroit. His mother worked as a housekeeper for wealthy families and noticed that all these homes had shelves and shelves stuffed with books. She realized then that these financially successful families had something in common: They all read. Although she herself couldn't read, she decided to instill a love of books in her children by simply encouraging them to read, read, read every day. This encouragement grew in each of her children into a drive to succeed, and all of them turned out to be highly accomplished. That encouragement to read was Carson's sixth man. He has received many merit awards for his work and contributions to the scientific and medical fields, and among them is the highest civilian award in the United States—the Presidential Medal of Freedom.

All influences are valid, but the sixth man is the kind that doesn't quit provoking you until you do something about it. It's an active kind of influence, while people tend to be passive because over time they may change and loosen their hold on you.

---

professionally, then chances are you will stay committed and disciplined. If your sphere of influence is discouraging or lacks interest in what you're doing, then you could lose your focus and churn out mediocre work.

BUILD ON YOUR INHERENT STRENGTHS AND TALENTS

Take a blank piece of paper and draw a vertical line right down the center. In one column, sign your name as many times as possible using your dominant hand. In the other column, do the same thing—only this time, use your nondominant hand.

Unless you are truly ambidextrous, the two sides of the paper look vastly different. One side is legible, while the other resembles a four-year-old's henpecking. How did it feel signing with your nondominant hand? Frustrating? Awkward? Tedious? Slow?

This feeling perfectly demonstrates the struggle of developing weaknesses rather than honing innate strengths. We're not saying you shouldn't improve weaknesses—by all means, do! In fact, the premise of this book is development. But building up the talents or inclinations that you already possess and that engage you should not take a back seat, either, because strengths-based improvement delivers a more engaging and sustainable reward.

Take an introverted young CFO, for example. She prefers to work independently so that she can focus on her tasks. But her boss, the autocratic system CEO, wants her to start presenting financial reports twice a year to the system and hospital boards. Pronto! He doesn't give her enough time to prepare nor considers her ability to present. She is panicked because she hates public speaking and collaborating with other departments and staffs. Her new responsibility means she has to take public speaking classes and then prepare slides and practice before each presentation—on top of performing all of her other duties. Normally, she's confident, highly competent, and is a finance wizard. During her presentations, though, she sweats and stutters and second-guesses herself when she is asked a question. Because of all the time she spends on her presentations, her regular job begins to suffer. After just three presentations, she quits her job.

That's a total waste of talent!

Before you can hone your strengths, you have to accurately identify them. How do you do that? Here are some simple, straightforward methods:

1. Ask for feedback from your sphere of influence and other trusted sources.

2. Look through past performance reviews, and focus on areas in which you excelled.

3. Observe yourself at work for at least one week and take notes. What gets you excited? What grabs your attention or piques your interest? What do you find most rewarding? What puts you in a steady state of "don't bother me, I'm doing something"?

4. Take an aptitude or competency test. One powerful tool is the StrengthsFinder. Don Clifton—founder of the Clifton StrengthsFinder, Gallup's online psychological assessment—is known as the father of the strengths-based movement. The catalyst of this movement was a 1950s research study on a speed-reading course. The study found that the greatest growth in ability occurred among students who were already reading at an above-average rate of speed. The average readers started at 90 words per minute (wpm) and the speed-reading course improved their speed to 150 wpm, an increase of 67 percent. The above-average readers, on the other hand, started at 350 wpm and went up to 2,900 wpm, an improvement of about 800 percent!

    The StrengthsFinder tool is based on the idea that you have the most opportunity to improve in areas in which you are already strong. For example, if you're highly analytical, you have a better chance of deepening that expertise than someone who has average analytical abilities. Similarly, if you're a natural people person, you are better at building and strengthening relationships and connections than someone who is independent. Find the StrengthsFinder tool here: www.strengthsfinder.com/home.aspx. For another method, see Exhibit 6.2.

The more you refine your talents and focus on the things you do well (instead of poorly), the more confident you become and the better your overall performance gets (even in areas that don't come naturally to you). The reverse is also true: The more you beat yourself up over your weaknesses and your deficiencies, the lower your self-esteem gets and the more mistakes you commit.

Exhibit 6.2 Better Than 10,000 Others

"What do you do better than 10,000 others?" This is a question Laurie often poses during her consulting sessions. The typical first response is, "Are you kidding?! I have nothing that special to offer." But with a little prodding, attendees begin to share with their small groups. And then something beautiful happens. The room comes alive with the din of chatter and exchange of ideas. Instead of individuals talking about their personal strengths, group members heap praises on each other:

- "Donna is such a deep well of knowledge. Every time I have a complex patient case, I always ask her."

- "Robin is so beloved by our patients. The first question out of their mouths is, 'Where's Robin?'"

- "Erika is so good at solving problems. When the network server crashes or the EHR software is not responding, Erika can troubleshoot and get us right back on track."

Do you know why it's so hard for people to answer this question? Often, we only hear the complaints about our performance or an exhortation to work on our weak areas. We seldom hear praises for what we did right. Is it any wonder, then, that people don't think they outperform even two other people, let alone 10,000?!

Remember These

- Being a follower is an act of active participation.
- Followers "actually contribute more than 80 percent to the success of any project, any organization, while leaders at best contribute only 20 percent."
- Culture can be defined as "the way we do things around here."
- "Kill the snake" means if you see a problem, fix it. It's about taking ownership.
- The company you keep has the power to strengthen or weaken your performance. If your sphere of influence is supportive and enthusiastic about your efforts to grow personally and professionally, then chances are you will stay committed and disciplined. If your sphere of influence is discouraging or lacks interest in what you're doing, then you could lose your focus and churn out mediocre work.
- Building up the talents that you already possess and that engage you should not take a back seat to improving your weaknesses because strengths-based improvement delivers a more engaging and sustainable reward.

REFERENCES

Kelley, R. E. 1992. *The Power of Followership: How to Create Leaders People Want to Follow and Followers Who Lead Themselves.* New York: Doubleday.

Sorensen, A. 2014. Personal communication with the authors, April.

ADDITIONAL RESOURCES

Atchison, T. A. 2003. *Followership: A Practical Guide to Aligning Leaders and Followers*. Chicago: Health Administration Press.

Bass, B. M., and R. E. Riggio. 2008. *Transformational Leadership*. Mahwah, NJ: Lawrence Erlbaum Associates, Inc.

Kelley, R. E. 1988. "In Praise of Followers." *Harvard Business Review*. http://hbr.org/1988/11/in-praise-of-followers/ar/1.

Rath, T. 2007. *StrengthsFinder 2.0*. Lincoln, NE: Gallup Press.

Rath, T., and B. Conchie. 2009. *Strengths-Based Leadership 2.0*. Lincoln, NE: Gallup Press.

Note to My 25-Year-Old Self

Looking back over my career, I reflect on the great privilege it has been to serve organizations that had a mission and values that were aligned with my personal mission and values. The opportunity to be part of a calling that is larger than me provides immeasurable enrichment. We in healthcare are particularly fortunate to serve others at their time of greatest need. Very early in my career, as an administrative resident, I had two mentors whose values were wholly focused on serving the patient and the greater good, using the organization's resources. The selfless example of others who went before me served to guide my own path. I advise emerging leaders today to seek to work for an organization whose mission and values are congruent with their own.

My words of wisdom to my 25-year-old self would be to *achieve* more work–life balance. Take time and be present with family and friends, and invest in self-renewal. This is challenging when serving a 24/7 mission. That being said, your organization will be better served when you are fully engaged at both home and work.

As you advance in your career, you will be called upon to make increasingly difficult decisions. Exercising good judgment requires sound values, solid preparation, and an effective and ready team. Your team may include employees, your board of directors or key advisors, and your family. Surround yourself with great people who will hold you accountable. Encourage others, and ask them to encourage you.

Lead by example. Seek to learn, grow, and succeed, but do so with mindfulness toward balance and prudence. This is a time of great change in our industry, compounded by rapidly increasing technology and accessibility. Leverage the technology available to you, but make time to unplug and recharge. If you're stressed out all the time, you'll make more mistakes and may not interact with your team as effectively as you could. As a leader, if you don't take time for yourself and your family and friends, it can send a message or expectation that others cannot take that needed time either.

While planning your career and considering strategic transitions, seek wise counsel from advisors, colleagues, and mentors. Listen, consider, and then trust your instincts. In 1981, I was an associate administrator in a large hospital of a multihospital system. I was presented with an opportunity to become the CEO of a 60-bed rural hospital in the system. Most of my advisors felt that it would be a mistake, that I wouldn't advance from there. But it felt like the right choice, and I followed my gut. After one year (of having the best time of my career), I was reassigned—this time as CEO of a 400-bed community hospital in the system. I don't believe that would have happened if I hadn't demonstrated experience leading as CEO of a smaller facility. Ultimately, you have to do what you feel is best. You own your own career. Reflect, consider where you feel called, where you can best serve, and make a difference. I am grateful for the support of my family to make moves and transitions throughout my career. Don't look back and regret. Make courageous and strategic decisions.

Be yourself. Discover and understand your strengths and weaknesses. Surround yourself with people who buttress your limitations. Embrace diversity of thought, and be intentional to seek out those with contrasting experience, expertise, and perspective. Be transparent in your weaknesses, and empower others to contribute where you are less disposed. Your authenticity will engender the trust and confidence of those around you. Seek candid feedback on how you can improve as a leader, and set an example and expectation that others do the same.

Be engaged in your profession. Affiliation and involvement in the American College of Healthcare Executives (ACHE) has been invaluable in equipping me as a leader. ACHE offers tremendous professional education and development resources, publications, and tools that increase effectiveness. Its board certification process equips and validates your credibility. For me, however, the most powerful value of ACHE is the network of colleagues it offers. I've met people who have helped me develop my network, who have been my best and most candid advisors, and who were there when I have faced challenges. I heartily encourage you to engage and advance.

Signed,
William C. Schoenhard, LFACHE
Chairman (2006–2007), American College of Healthcare Executives
Former (Retired) Deputy Undersecretary for Health for Operations and Management, US Department of Veterans Affairs

CHAPTER 7

Try, or Find Inspiration in, Servant Leadership

"Good leaders must first become good servants."

—Robert K. Greenleaf, Founder, Greenleaf Center for Servant Leadership

---

Reading Points

- The Benefits of Servant Leadership

- The Unassuming Acts of Servant Leaders

- Choosing to Be Brave, Not Popular

- Joining or Starting Difficult Conversations

WHAT KIND OF leader do you want to be? There are many leadership styles you can try and choose from. But if you want to be a leader who has a reputation for putting other people first, then it's time you look into servant leadership.

Servant leadership might as well be called *selfless leadership*. Because it isn't about you. It's about your audience, your stakeholders, your constituents (yep, like a politician; did you know every healthcare leader has a dual role as a politician?). These constituents include the organization's senior leaders, board of directors, management, employees (including your staff, if you have them), patients and their families, physicians, and community members and business leaders. It's only about you in the sense that you are the one doing the serving. As such, you have to commit to serving the needs and wants of others to help them become extraordinary.

Just like everything else in the book, being a servant leader takes years, which is likely why this style is mostly associated with senior leaders. But you can begin this journey now. There is enormous value in serving your stakeholders in the early years of your career.

So how can you get started?

First, practice the strategies we offer in this and other chapters. We say this not to give lip service to our own recommendations but to drive home the point that many of the concepts we discuss—like self-awareness, humility, personal growth or learning, commitment and self-discipline, followership, integrity, and building trust and relationships—share the same philosophy with servant leadership. Each of these strategies will get you closer to becoming a servant leader.

Second, be kind—or at the very least, be nice. Simple as that. You don't have to be a saint, but you do have to be considerate, courteous, helpful, and modest with everyone you deal with. Keep in mind that hiring managers also look for this character trait. They don't want to recruit and select job candidates who don't care, are arrogant, are selfish, or are rude. After all, it is much easier to teach skills to kind people than to teach kindness to skilled but mean people.

In this chapter, we continue to share improvement techniques we've learned from our more-than-15-years' experience in healthcare. But this time, we've set our eyes on practices that are intended to bring out the servant leader in you.

THE BENEFITS OF SERVANT LEADERSHIP

Let's be clear on one thing: True servant leaders have altruistic intentions. They are servants not because they get money, power, prestige, or any other perks from it. They are servants because they see serving as a critical duty or responsibility (Greenleaf 1977). They provide encouragement, approval, resources, information, other necessary support, and even tough love so that employees can do their jobs and do them well and so that the community/society can benefit.

This doesn't mean servant leadership offers no benefits for the person. One benefit is genuine influence, the kind that inspires (*not* requires) others to follow your vision, to be loyal to you, to perform their best work, and to become servant leaders themselves. You can't buy, take, or beg for that kind of influence. You have to earn it. Never, ever assume that having a title (as a CEO, COO, Executive VP, or CFO, for example) automatically means having genuine influence. No matter where you are in the organizational chart, influence is golden. But it's invaluable as your career progresses and when you reach the executive level because that's when more complicated decisions that require more stakeholder buy-in are made.

Another benefit of servant leadership is better reputation. Reputation is what other people think of you. You have no direct control over it. What you can control is your own behavior. If you act selflessly—for example, being a team player, volunteering to help, and supporting others' work and goals—people will notice. That's when their opinion of you will improve, their trust and respect for you grows, and your credibility goes up. Then, these same people will spread the word, guaranteeing that your reputation precedes you wherever you go. Of course, if you behave selfishly, word will spread faster—but not in a good way.

We've said this before, and we'll say it again: The little acts you commit every day matter, and they compound over time to create a big change or outcome. If you adopt servant leadership now—now that the stakes are lower than if you were a titled executive—you will see in a few years (perhaps even months) that your influence has grown exponentially among those you serve day in and day out. Even if you change jobs or move on to another organization later in your career, your habit of serving others will be beneficial in so many ways.

THE UNASSUMING ACTS OF SERVANT LEADERS

Exercise these servant leader acts until they turn into habits.

Never Ask Someone Else to Do Something That You Yourself Can't or Won't Do

Intimidated to approach the CFO about a complicated budget question or an overdue report? Don't send a team member on your behalf. Won't lie or cover up for anyone's mistake? Don't even insinuate to anyone to do the same for you when you mess up. Nothing says selfish or self-serving more than refusing to do or face a difficult, awkward, or potentially risky task and pushing it on to be somebody else's problem. That's cowardice and abuse of power that people don't easily forget or forgive.

Another way of exercising this tiny act is to always be willing to roll up your sleeves and pitch in when needed. Servant leaders never think they are too high up the totem pole or too successful to do menial tasks or manual labor. They don't assign those tasks to their direct reports, and they are not content with just supervising the work; instead, they get involved and are happy for the opportunity to literally (not figuratively) get their hands dirty. Boxing emergency packages for the community after a natural disaster, answering phones on the patient care floor during a staff shortage or an unusually high patient census, and offering your expertise to help solve or prevent a problem are just some ways you can show you are not above doing things outside your official duties.

Say Yes to Every Opportunity to Help or Participate

By doing so, you are exposing yourself to new experiences and possibilities; learning about different roles, departments, settings, and processes; and meeting leaders and staff you would not encounter otherwise. Most important, you are creating goodwill between you and those you're serving. Immerse yourself in these experiences, and absorb as much of their lessons as possible. Even (and especially) if an initiative or project doesn't turn out as planned, you can learn something that you can apply later.

Communicate Clearly and Regularly

Whether you're leading a big project team, supervising a small staff, or just going about your daily tasks, direct and regular communication is a service you're performing. How? When you speak clearly (and listen!), give simple instructions, define roles and expectations, share relevant information, provide and request updates, or check on progress and problems, you are empowering all involved in the project or in the exchange—whether staff members, bosses, doctors, or vendors and consultants—to do their part. Your communication is a guide, something for them to work with and work toward. Without communication, the work stalls, misunderstanding multiplies, mistakes are made and aren't fixed, deadlines are ignored, and people get very angry. Plus, when you communicate, you're showing that you care and that you're there when people need you.

Don't Be Afraid to Ask the Question

Six little words can have a huge impact on your reputation or others' opinion of you. And no, they aren't, "May I have a pay raise?" Those words are "Can you help me to understand?" Admitting you don't understand something is hard. But in showing that you don't know and that you need help, you gain not only the knowledge you need but also strong allies.

Don't underestimate the power of humility and vulnerability. When you admit that you don't fully understand something, the barriers between employees (no matter their titles) immediately disintegrate. There is no faster way to a completely neutral, healthy, and productive discussion—and to move the conversation forward—than posing this question. Plus, it allows others to be of service to you. Who among us doesn't enjoy using our know-how to come to someone's aid? Who isn't flattered when asked to lend our expertise? This is especially true of healthcare professionals, who have built our lives around serving others.

Take this story as an example:

A hospital COO we know has made asking this question a habit. His background is nontraditional: He earned his stripes in the marketing and strategic planning realm of healthcare. He had limited exposure to the operational and clinical sides. Because of this background, others were often quick to dismiss him, unsure of his credibility. At first, he reacted by being defensive. He even doubted his own abilities. But then he developed a better approach. He began to ask, "Can you help me to understand?" It was such a simple request, but it disarmed those he was talking to and led them to serve, teach, and collaborate rather than doubt and attack. He genuinely won them over.

Is the question scary? You bet! Worth it? Oh yeah.

CHOOSING TO BE BRAVE, NOT POPULAR

We all want to be liked. It's human nature. Because of that, at work you may be tempted to make everyone happy so that you can be liked. The danger of caving in to this temptation is that you may soften the blow of bad news, fail to set performance expectations for your employees or team members, share information that is not intended for disclosure, or turn a blind eye to bad behavior or abuses of power (especially by your work friends). These acts are directly opposite from those practiced by servant leaders, who are experts at building relationships but savvy with not crossing boundaries.

Did you know that what gets you liked in the long run often involves making the unpopular, nerve-racking decisions in the short run? Focus on that long game. That's where the payoff is. Don't let a self-centered desire to be liked drive your professional decisions. If the motivation for your decisions is simply to "make nice"—not because you have the best interests of the organization, its employees, and the community at heart—then you're doing everyone (including you) a disservice. Sure, you won't rock the boat this way, but you will certainly undermine your authority (not to mention your career down the road).

Instead of being liked, work toward being respected. Respect is equity that you earn through good behavior, service, hard work, and accomplishment. You could easily lose that equity, however. For example, discretion is crucial in leadership, and a breach of that discretion leads to loss of respect. If you share confidential or inside information to endear someone to you, that individual is looking at you as a person who cannot be trusted, not as a person who is open and honest. Any respect you've earned from that person vanishes at that point.

Hold Others to High Standards

Having earned a Division 1 athletic scholarship, Natalie was sure she was ready for college-level track practice. And then she met her coach, a hard-driving but highly respected leader. His team's respect for him ran so deep that all members pushed themselves beyond their personal limits to win meets or perform at their best. During his rigorous practices, Natalie would run off the track to throw up from exhaustion. She would quickly compose herself and then return to finish her workout. That happened a few times, especially in her first semester of college. The coach (and his coaches) didn't tolerate excuses or complaints, nor did he care whether the team liked his decisions. He knew what every athlete on his team was capable of, and he held each of them to very high standards. Despite his toughness, everyone clearly understood that he was coming from a good place: He only wanted what was best for the team and the individual athletes; he wasn't doing it for his own good. Natalie pushed through the long, grueling practices and became efficient at writing term papers on the long bus rides to and from meets. Her self-discipline, tenacity, and time management skills—not to mention her physical fitness and running times—only got better because of this experience. All thanks to a brave coach who wasn't afraid to make the unpopular decisions that serve the interests of his athletes.

Just like the coach, Laurie's science teacher in high school was demanding. She wasn't adored by her students, and her teaching style was an acquired taste. She refused to let anyone slack off. But she knew science and was adamant that every student learned it. What Laurie didn't realize until many years later was that this teacher wasn't tough because she was mean spirited. In fact, quite the opposite: She was difficult because she cared a lot about the students' future. She pushed them to turn in their best work and to think critically. She drilled into them not just scientific principles but also discipline and structure. These are principles that contributed to Laurie's growth and stay with her today.

Like the coach and the science teacher, you should hold your constituents (not to mention yourself) to a higher standard. It's not easy to do, and you certainly will not win any popularity contests and you may feel left out. But as a future leader, you have to start making the tough calls for the benefit of the people you serve (not just for your benefit). That will earn you respect, which has a much better value than being liked. We're not asking you to be icy or hostile; in fact, we encourage you to be warm and caring. What we're asking you to be is courageous—to do the right things for the greatest number of people.

JOINING OR STARTING DIFFICULT CONVERSATIONS

"If you're not at the table, you can bet you're on the menu." Have you heard that saying before? It's silly, but it makes a great point. If you don't start or join the difficult conversation, you will be counted out.

When (never *if*) you fail or make a mistake, the next steps should include a discussion about what went wrong, what you did and didn't do, and how it can be prevented next time. This is a difficult, awkward conversation that you may delay, avoid, or skip. And we can't blame you; we know what that's like. (See Chapter 8 for more discussion on failure.)

But if you keep stalling this conversation, what would your constituents say about you? Would they start to doubt your ability to lead and serve them? Postponing it doesn't make the issues disappear. In fact, they undoubtedly will only get worse.

What do you think would happen if you do sit down at the table? You may get an earful, sure. But criticism to your face is always better than criticism behind your back. Be prepared to approach the meeting with humility, and answer questions, apologize, take ownership, and offer solutions. The conversation will end soon enough, and you'll feel relieved and proud for having faced the music once and for all. Plus, you'll come away with some lessons learned, and you'll certainly earn the respect of your team, staff, and even boss just for showing up.

Joining or starting difficult conversations (whether related to failures or something else) is a test of your commitment to serve. If you step up, you've passed. You're sending a message to others that, despite your fears of confrontations and despite setbacks that happen, you're there to continue your service and there when you're needed most.

Servant leaders don't quit when the going gets tough. Neither should you.

Remember These

- Servant leadership isn't about you. It's about your audience, your stakeholders, your constituents.

- Being a servant leader takes years, which is likely why this style is mostly associated with senior leaders. But you can begin this journey now. There is enormous value in serving your stakeholders in the early years of your career.

- Many of the concepts we discuss—like self-awareness, humility, personal growth or learning, commitment and self-discipline, followership, integrity, and building trust and relationships—share the same philosophy with servant leadership. Each of these strategies will get you closer to becoming a servant leader.

- Be nice. Simple as that. You don't have to be a saint, but you do have to be considerate, courteous, helpful, and modest with everyone you deal with. Keep in mind that hiring managers also look for this character trait.

- True servant leaders have altruistic intentions. They are servants not because they get money, power, prestige,

→

or any other perks from it. They are servants because they see serving as a critical duty or responsibility.

- One benefit of being a servant leader is genuine influence, the kind that inspires (*not* requires) others to follow your vision, to be loyal to you, to perform their best work, and to become servant leaders themselves.

- Another benefit of servant leadership is a better reputation. Reputation is what other people think of you. If you act selflessly—for example, being a team player, volunteering to help, and supporting others' work and goals—people will notice. That's when their opinion of you will improve, their trust and respect for you grows, and your credibility goes up.

REFERENCE

Greenleaf, R. 1977. *Servant Leadership*. Mahwah, NJ: Paulist Press.

CHAPTER 8

Bounce Back from Failure

"Mistakes are the usual bridge between
inexperience and wisdom."

—*Phyllis Theroux, Essayist*

Reading Points

- Managing Failure
- Taking and Handling Criticism
- Persevering Through the Nos
- Trying New Things
- Forgetting

- Michael Jordan was cut from his high school basketball team.
- Walt Disney was fired from a newspaper for "lacking imagination" and "having no original ideas."
- Steve Jobs was unceremoniously removed from the company he started.

- Oprah Winfrey was demoted from her job as a news anchor because she "wasn't fit for television."
- The Beatles were rejected by a recording studio, which said, "We don't like their sound, they have no future in show business."

THIS LIST COULD go on and on, but our point is this: Failures happen to everyone, even to very talented, famous people. As we've said, failures are a matter of when, never a matter of if. All we can do is hope for the best, but plan for the worst.

Don't define your career in this constantly changing, high-stress, high-stakes healthcare industry by the number of times you failed or made a mistake. Doing so is unfair, and it diminishes the countless things you've accomplished, contributed, and improved. Instead, see failure for what it is—an inevitable and scary occurrence that you can bounce back and learn from and you can prevent. How you overcome or rebound from adversity is what should define your career, because that's tough work that not only requires but also shows your strength of character—whether you're tenacious, resilient, committed, disciplined, progress oriented, and so on.

Many of us were schooled to believe that failure is bad. But that's only true if you let it stop you from trying again. In fact, failure is good because it provides learning and growth opportunities. It also promotes taking risks by applying new approaches to old or existing processes. The corporate giant 3M, for example, has a company-wide philosophy that encourages employees to fail—and do so regularly (Kalb 2013). If employees aren't failing 95 percent of the time, the company reasons, then they likely aren't trying anything fresh and current. Although we elevate our chances of falling flat on our faces if the new techniques don't work, the fact that we ventured out to test new waters is valuable. It expands not only our skills but also our professional and personal horizons.

In this chapter, we challenge you to rethink your ideas about failure. We provide tips for managing failure, facing criticism and rising above it, and persevering despite rejections.

MANAGING FAILURE

Early careerists who are new to healthcare enjoy a grace period (although this varies from organization to organization) in which they are afforded some leeway to learn their roles and responsibilities and to adjust to the environment. This "honeymoon" period is a great time for you to establish good habits, including managing failure or what to do when you make a mistake.

During this time, when you are eager to pursue projects, participate in activities, and prove yourself, the likelihood that you will fail at least once is high. If it does happen, stay calm. It's not the end of the world. Handle the situation as graciously, humbly, and professionally as you can. The grace you show at this time will be noted by your colleagues, bosses, and even patients or their families. More important, it will set you up to successfully handle more complicated failures as your career progresses.

Here are our suggested ways to manage failure:

- *Admit your part in the failure.* Acknowledging your mistake, often publicly, is the only way you can begin to learn and to pick up the broken pieces and start over. An admission requires bravery and humility, as there will be a lot of criticisms of your actions and scrutiny of your work processes. Explain and share information, and listen more than talk.

- *Reject rejection.* As painful and disappointing as a failure is, it shouldn't have so much power that it paralyzes you emotionally and mentally. Don't allow that to happen.

Dwell on it if you must, but don't dwell too long. The more time you spend on beating yourself up, the less time you spend on recovering, learning, and moving on. Bounce back!

- *Put failure in perspective.* Failure is a temporary, isolated setback. Many (if not most) of the workplace mistakes you make are one-time events, not patterns. If resolved appropriately, they don't spread to other parts or cause permanent damage. If you learned from them and committed to not repeating them, they don't recur. Have some perspective. If you see every failure as a career-ending, reputation-ruining event, you are only elevating your fear.

- *See failure as part of the success process.* There's no such thing as an overnight success. Even those who won the lottery bought tickets for years before they hit the jackpot. When we landed our respective executive jobs at an early age, we had been paying dues formally and informally for several years to position ourselves for the next big thing. Success not only takes time but also involves failure—a lot of them. When you view failure as just another part of the success process, like acing a job interview and getting a promotion, then you're taking away its power to rule you; you're putting yourself in charge of it. Embrace it. Failing is far better than going stale in your career because you won't take a risk at doing something new.

- *Try something new.* After a mistake, be brave and try a completely different approach. You've heard of that quote attributed to Albert Einstein: "The definition of insanity is doing the same thing over and over again and expecting different results." Don't fall in that category. While it's ok to make mistakes, it's *not* ok to keep repeating the same mistakes. Do whatever it takes to prevent that from happening.

- *Reflect in the aftermath of failure.* Was your mistake a competency error? A political faux pas? The result of negligence? Do you need more training or practice? Do you need a better understanding of emotional intelligence and spheres of influence, for example? When you evaluate what happened, be honest with yourself. Think of the kinds of mistakes you tend to make and home in on the causes and solutions. Career advancement can be made on the heels of a mistake or a rejection (we discuss this point later), as long as you commit to learning from each failure and never repeating it.

TAKING AND HANDLING CRITICISM

Generally speaking, the higher your leadership position is, the more visible you are inside and outside the organization. The greater your visibility, the more critics you have and the more heat you must be willing to take. Everyone is scrutinizing your every move and feels entitled to share their opinions about your performance, decisions, behavior, character, associations or relationships, successes, and failures. You get called out for the things you did and didn't do. You get both wanted and unwanted, constructive and mean-spirited feedback. You get blamed for every problem and scolded for every solution that doesn't pan out. The negative attention can be relentless. And all of these happen privately and publicly, online and offline.

If you're uncomfortable with this barrage of criticism and feedback, now is a good time for you to grow thick skin and broad shoulders. You're gonna need them not only when you reach the C-suite but also as you make your way there. While we can't give you thick skin and broad shoulders, we can offer you advice on how to receive, view, and handle criticism, especially after a failure.

Essentially, people receive three kinds of criticisms: (1) the angry or edgy comments that sting, admonish, demand, scare, shame, or belittle; (2) the constructive feedback that informs, teaches, corrects, recommends improvements, points out weaknesses, and encourages; and (3) a combination of the two. Expect all kinds of criticism. Your boss may give it to you, and so may your team members and even complete strangers. As we said in Chapter 7, step up to these difficult conversations.

When receiving criticism, be open and self-reflective. There's a little truth in everything. Don't immediately label as useless the feedback from a source you think has absolutely nothing to do with you. You might find nuggets of wisdom, no matter how tiny, in what that critic says. Don't dismiss the lessons from or the perspective of people you don't like or who are especially critical of you. Embrace all critiques and feedback. They give you fresh insights into, for example, why the failure took place, what areas you need to fix or approaches you need to adopt to prevent the same mistake, and how you can help yourself and others bounce back.

Three things can help you take and handle criticisms in general:

1. *Personal development.* This includes but is certainly not limited to reading life-affirming books, listening to uplifting audiobooks or podcasts, and surrounding yourself with positive people. The happier you are, the less likely you are to be bothered by criticism.

2. *Self-awareness.* Being aware of your strengths and weaknesses gives you confidence. It's not arrogance, but self-esteem—the feeling of being okay with who you are despite your flaws. This confidence allows you to process criticisms without getting emotionally and psychologically wrecked by the comments.

3. *Coaching.* Many high performers rely on coaches. Elite athletes have position coaches, strength and conditioning

coaches, and sports psychologists. Professional musicians and vocalists have teachers and instructors. Leaders in various industries hire executive coaches. Why approach coaches instead of your sphere of influence for this purpose? Professional coaches provide objective inputs and resources, unlike biased and loyal friends and colleagues. Coaches routinely give feedback and critique elements of performance, making their clients immune to and responsive to the critique process. We're not saying those clients don't feel the sting and anxiety of regular criticism, but they have an acute understanding that the feedback is not a personal attack but a tool to coax out their best performance.

See Exhibit 8.1 for strategies for handling unsolicited criticism.

PERSEVERING THROUGH THE NOS

You may not know who Cordia Harrington is, but chances are you know her product. Cordia's business, The Bun Company, makes the bread used by McDonald's, Kentucky Fried Chicken, and Chili's (among other major enterprises). This was not always the case, though. Cordia approached McDonald's 33 times before the restaurant chain said "yes" to her product. Thirty-three times!

How many nos do you need to hear before you stop asking the question? Before you throw in the proverbial towel? We'd bet that your threshold for rejection is lower than you think. That's because we live in an instant-gratification society, where if we don't get immediate results or an immediate yes, we get discouraged. If we get discouraged, we tend to give up.

But anything worth having is worth doing and is worth the wait, so keep going even when you hear that no, even if you're rejected many times. Persevere, as Cordia did; try other routes, as

Exhibit 8.1 How to Handle Unsolicited Criticism

It's one thing to ask and receive feedback from your network contacts and other work associates. It's another to get unsolicited criticisms. Resist the temptation to defend yourself against them. With these steps, you can transform the negative into something productive:

- *Listen.* You may be quick to interrupt or state your case. Stop. Hold on. Absorb what the person with the beef has to say. Wait for them to finish, just as you would want if the tables were turned.

- *Consider the source.* Does this person have a genuine grievance? Or is he or she just jealous? Does this person have a track record of being insubordinate? To answer this question, you may need to reach out to your mentors, network contacts, or an objective party you respect. Ask them about the alleged critic and criticism. Find out if the criticism is truly justified.

- *Don't take it personally.* This may well be the hardest tip to follow. It's natural to take criticisms personally; after all, it's your brand out there on the line. Resist that urge. Maintain objectivity as much as you can. Otherwise, you won't get anything good out of this experience, only bad.

- *Stay calm.* Take a deep breath. One of the worst things you can do is be reactive and lash out. You need presence of mind to explore whether or not this criticism is founded.

- *Ask clarifying questions.* If a blanket criticism is made ("You never respond to my e-mails!"), you'll feel like it doesn't hold much water. Ask for specifics, details about where you allegedly went wrong. You can objectively judge if the criticism has merit only if you have these details. And you most certainly can't remedy the situation if you don't have the specifics about what you did wrong in the first place.

- *Take ownership.* If you really have wronged someone or some people, you need to own up to it. Apologize, and do it properly. (See Chapter 3 for a longer discussion of apologies.) Personal accountability and humility are some of the hallmark characteristics of exceptional leaders.

- *Embrace the message.* As a leader, you are in the seemingly counterintuitive position of valuing criticism. Because of your position, it's only natural that people will have a beef with you from time to time. You need to look at this as almost an honor, that people are so invested in the team or the organization that they are willing

(continued)

to put themselves on the line to make that, perhaps, brash opinion. You just may have something to learn from this critique. You never know, there could be beautiful rewards in the end when you address the criticism.

- *Take action.* Yes, you need to do more than just nod and speak to the criticism. You need to act on it. Value that feedback or experience as an opportunity to grow professionally as a leader. If you grow from this difficult experience, you are unlikely to find yourself in the same situation again. Good for you, your team, and your entire organization.

Ultimately, how you respond to unsolicited criticisms is what makes you stand out from other emerging leaders. Seize the opportunity to turn the negative into a positive.

Laurie did (see her story below); and be gracious in the process, as Natalie was (see her story below as well).

Laurie's first healthcare job post-college was as an administrative assistant in a large health system. She had no desire to stay in the role long term, so she started applying for roles both inside and outside the organization. In the two years she held the job, she was passed over for two internal promotions and two external interviews for similar positions. If you're counting, that's four rejections! It was at this point that she began to grow very discouraged. And impatient.

She could have thrown in the towel, but she stuck it out. In the end, her persistence resulted in a defining point in her career. Through a mentoring relationship she had developed, a seasoned executive offered her a role as vice president of clinics for a community hospital. She was 22 at the time. Landing the position more than tripled her salary. But more important, it gave her this priceless opportunity to advance her healthcare career and her leadership development.

The two years she endured getting rejected but refusing to back down felt like an eternity. But in reality, that period was barely more than a blip on the radar of her career.

When Natalie applied for her first CEO role, she initially was rejected. She wasn't considered for the final round of interviews because she lacked the five years of experience required for the job. When the hiring committee narrowed the field to four candidates, she was not selected as one of the four. Although disappointed, she took the decision in stride and wrote a follow-up thank you note to the board and the hiring committee. This impressed them, among other things.

Fast-forward two weeks. One of the candidates dropped out of contention and took another job. This opened up space for the committee to reach out to Natalie to give her an opportunity to interview. And she gave the interview of her young life. How did it turn out? Really well.

At 29 years old, Natalie became the CEO of a rural hospital. But had she adopted a defeatist, "sour grapes" attitude about the initial rejection, she might not have gotten a call back and missed out on her second chance.

Maximizing the Time In Between the No and the Yes

The first few years of your career seem to have a comparatively small impact on your overall career path, but this period is crucial to your development. This is the time to become stronger personally and professionally. This is the time to get tough. Ask yourself what you can do during this time to best position yourself when an opportunity comes along.

- *Be patient.* It's hard, *really* hard. Have confidence that your education, skills, and experiences have prepared you for the next level, but keep pursuing continual growth. Know that the right things will happen in your career when they're supposed to.
- *Look inward.* What are you doing with this experience? How do you apply the feedback and criticism you've

received to better equip yourself for the next job? Instead of looking at others who seem to have it so easy, or even those who may have landed the position you wanted, look inside you. See what you're doing to improve your chances of getting a yes. Often, a yes is simply beyond your control, but not always.

- *Work on your mental tenacity.* At some point during the 33 nos, even Cordia probably wondered if something was wrong with her. We know how disheartening that must have been, and we experienced just a fraction of the rejection she was up against. But she held strong and has become an inspiration for (even the envy of) many entrepreneurs and fledgling executives. That's mental tenacity!

- Mental tenacity is a rarely discussed trait of successful people, including leaders. It's not the same as mental discipline, which is being in control of how you think about and respond to situations (see Chapter 4). It's the dogged, stubborn determination in the face of critics, naysayers, personal shortcoming, and other seemingly insurmountable obstacles. It's not about being emotionally bulletproof, as if your feelings don't get hurt when you fail or get rejected. It's about going for it anyway.

- When you're mentally tenacious, you get better if you get a no. You don't surrender, you don't throw in the towel. One day, you can stash that towel away; you won't be needing it.

TRYING NEW THINGS

Somewhere around one year of age, most children try to walk. And after taking the first or second wobbly step (perhaps even before then), every one of those children falls. Some of them pick themselves back up like nothing happened. While others stay down and cry until they're ready to try again. They all go through this cycle of falling and getting up (and crying) many, many times. Then one day, success! They're walking—without wobbliness, without tears, without assistance from their parents. And then they move on to trying other things like running, going up and down stairs, climbing trees and tall objects, and riding a bike.

Children follow their natural curiosity. They find something of interest, and they explore it without fear of failure or pressure of success. How did we, as adults, lose so much of our childhood explorer mentality? Why are we so unwilling to take risks on new things, make mistakes or get rejected in the process, and recover only to try again?

If you've never failed, it doesn't mean you're better than everyone else. It means you're either incredibly lucky or not going beyond your comfort zone. But if you want that dream job, go big! Get creative with your approach. Do something you've never done before. Explore all your options, and try as many of them as possible. Don't be intimidated by failure, criticism, and rejection. Be brave and tenacious, just like a child learning to walk.

FORGETTING

Usually, forgetting (where we put our keys or the name of an old acquaintance, for example) is considered a bad thing, a sign of advancing age or mental fogginess. But sometimes forgetting or selective memory can be an asset. Here's why.

After failure or rejection, bouncing back to performing at your highest level is much easier if you can forget (read: stop thinking about) what knocked you down in the first place. Remembering the details is critical during a debriefing and during self-reflection after the fact—so that you can trace where things went wrong and so that you don't do the same thing again. But beyond that, replaying the details in your mind every day acts as a distraction and a detriment to your efforts to move forward.

Think about it this way: If a quarterback remembers the game-losing interception he threw during a big game *each time* he passes the football, do you think he'll ever lead his team to the Super Bowl? If a nurse replays in her head that fateful day she administered the wrong dosage to a patient *each time* she hands out medications, do you think she'll ever gain back her confidence so as not to repeat the medical error?

Professionals move on. They have to so that they can get back to doing what they love to do. If they don't, if they wallow in their failures or guilt or whatever psychological trauma they sustained, they will constantly second-guess themselves and weaken their performance. And poof, there goes their career.

As we said in the beginning of this chapter, you shouldn't define your career by your failures. You should define it by the way you overcame the adversity, by the way you bounced back and learned and thrived afterward.

"Failure?! What failure?"

Rookie Mistakes

Staying Psychologically Stuck

Failures can be devastating, as illustrated in this first-person account of Laurie's experience.

Shortly before the birth of my second child, I unexpectedly lost my company's only other employee under tragic circumstances. It was a tumultuous time, to say the least. I scrambled to perform and deliver for my clients, but ultimately I experienced some painful failures. And I let my clients down.

→

The workload spread between two employees now rested squarely on my eight-month-pregnant shoulders. I was managing the construction project of a medical office building for a physician group client, and the completion date was a mere five weeks away. Another client was in the final stages of recruiting a new physician and was revising its physician employment contract model.

During this time, I dropped a few balls, missed deadlines, and struggled to keep afloat. Seventy-two hours after the birth of my son, I was back in the office to meet a client's payroll audit deadline. I performed a construction punch-list with a sleeping newborn in tow. Many of my clients were incredibly understanding and accommodating, but a few were less tolerant. Not delivering on a promise is unacceptable to me, because I'm a driven, Type A person. My credibility and my company's reputation are my livelihood.

Four months later, I added two new colleagues to the team, and my business started to experience tremendous growth. In fact, we were in the very fortunate position of being able to double the staff size again to meet demand. But the residual impact of my recent failures remained. For me. Instead of finding the positive in these experiences and then moving past the negative, I allowed the failures to linger and mushroom. They psychologically devastated me.

I felt like a failure. My self-worth took a significant hit. Just as my business was starting to gain some traction, I was losing ground. Simply, I wasn't myself and, more important, I wasn't the leader the company needed at the time.

During these years, I was wrestling with the desire to pursue new business opportunities and devote myself more

→

exclusively to speaking and training. I kept thinking that if we just grew a bit more I would be freed up to do my own thing.

One word: delusional.

Despite our growth, I started to make decisions based on emotion. I was losing objectivity. I allowed one significant event to grab hold of me and let it dictate everything, when circumstances demanded stellar, committed, confident leadership.

Ultimately, I ended up dismantling the atomic bomb. I divested two major client relationships to two of my employees, who went on to form their own practice management consultancy. My other three employees accepted healthcare leadership roles elsewhere in the community. By the end of the following year, the transitions were complete. Without focus and passion for the company in its current construct, I was not capable of guiding its continued growth.

Now, I *know* that failures don't define us. And failures certainly aren't final—if you don't let them become the be-all, end-all. That truth, my friends, is easier said than lived. Unfortunate circumstances resulting in mistakes are as inevitable as taxes. Sure they hurt, but you've got to keep going regardless. Don't allow them to bring you down—not for a long time—because out of these challenges come opportunities to rise above in a way that, perhaps, wouldn't have been possible had you not developed the fortitude from a major setback.

Remember These

- Failures are a matter of when, never a matter of if. All we can do is hope for the best, but plan for the worst.

- Don't define your career in this constantly changing, high-stress, high-stakes healthcare industry by the number of times you failed or made a mistake. How you overcome or rebound from adversity is what should define your career, because that's tough work that not only requires but also shows your strength of character.

- Failure is good because it provides learning and growth opportunities. It also promotes taking risks by applying new approaches to old or existing processes.

- The higher your leadership position is, the more visible you are inside and outside the organization. The greater your visibility, the more critics you have and the more heat you must be willing to take.

- Don't dismiss the lessons from or the perspective of people you don't like or who are especially critical of you. Embrace all critiques and feedback.

- But anything worth having is worth doing and is worth the wait, so keep going even when you hear that no, even you're rejected many times.

- If you've never failed, it doesn't mean you're better than everyone else. It means you're either incredibly lucky or not going beyond your comfort zone.

REFERENCE

Kalb, I. 2013. "Innovation Isn't Just About Brainstorming New Ideas." *Business Insider*. Published July 8. www.businessinsider.com/innovate-or-die-a-mantra-for-every-business-2013-7.

CHAPTER 9

Network, Network, Network!

"Surround yourself with only people who are going to lift you higher."

—*Oprah Winfrey, TV Personality*

Reading Points

- Networking Done Right

- Networking for Introverts

- Network Up

- Networking According to Your Season of Life

SOME PROFESSIONALS MIGHT think that networking is a luxury they can't afford. "I'm too busy as it is!" they might say, justifying their decision to skip an industry event in which they could connect with hundreds of people. But networking is far from a luxury. It's a basic necessity that professionals can't afford to do without.

Want to raise your visibility and profile in your organization and beyond? You must network. Want to get the inside scoop on a position, change disciplines or enter a different field, get job offers, or make a lateral or vertical career move? You must network. Want to be introduced or exposed to those whose career path you admire? You must network. Plus, continual networking (read: developing rapport and serving your contacts) is beneficial even when you already have a job or don't have a specific need. Someday, you will need to tap into this network, and the relationships you've been building will already be there to lend you a hand.

Don't think that networking is only beneficial for early careerists and job seekers. It's also a go-to activity for mid-level professionals and senior executives who are continual learners, relationship builders, people persons, collaborators, communicators, innovators, strategists, and doers. They fully engage with their network for all kinds of reasons—from exchanging and testing ideas to discovering new approaches to problem solving to forming partnerships, to name just a very few. (See Exhibit 9.1 for two examples of how a simple networking relationship can evolve into a job offer and a partnership.)

Exhibit 9.1 Networking = More Working

From Colleague to Boss

For nine out of the ten years Laurie owned a consulting firm, she shared clients with John, a bank president. While she assisted her physician clients in launching their private practices, he assisted these same clients with their practices' financing and banking needs. He earned their business nearly every time, presenting strong responses to the requests for proposal and delivering valuable industry expertise and stellar customer service.

The two had mutual clients and worked on many shared projects over the years. During that time, Laurie's consultancy focus transitioned from healthcare management to leadership development and strengths-based leadership facilitation. John engaged her to work with his executive team and to facilitate a strengths retreat. Eventually, he offered to acquire a portion of her business and to create within his organization a unique position custom-made for Laurie. She would lead the bank's brand strategy, organizational culture, and healthcare banking division. The opportunity, though nontraditional, was a brilliant fit, bolstered by their

(continued)

mutual respect for each other's expertise, their rapport, and their years of supporting each other's business. Laurie jumped at the offer.

She didn't apply for the job; in fact, she wasn't even looking for jobs at all. Her consistent networking approach, however, brought her this opportunity and steered her toward a career path she could have never defined on her own.

When Natalie Met Laurie

In the spring of 2008, Laurie and Natalie were both attendees at ACHE's Leaders Conference in Phoenix. On day one of the conference, the presenter asked all 35 attendees to stand up one by one to introduce themselves. When Natalie got up and told the room she was the CEO of a hospital, Laurie thought, "Wow, she looks about my age. I need to introduce myself and get to know her." That afternoon during coffee break, Laurie did just that. They made plans to connect over dinner the following evening. They had a great conversation at dinner, and they both enjoyed and learned a lot from each other. On day three of the conference, they parted ways, having exchanged business cards.

One week later, Laurie called Natalie's office.

"Hey, this is Laurie Baedke. We just met in Phoenix, but would you have any interest in collaborating with me on an ACHE Congress session for early careerists around the concepts of professional development, networking, and career path design?"

"Is this that blonde woman I had dinner with a few weeks ago?" Natalie thought to herself, but aloud she said, "I'm interested, but when is it due? Tell me more!"

Inspiration was sparked and a plan was drafted. Three weeks later, they submitted a session proposal for Congress 2009. It was accepted. Now, six years later, the session is alive and well. It has even become this book.

Big business (as well as small business) is also in the networking game. Think Walmart, with its network of suppliers and distributors; Amazon, with its network of warehouses; and Apple, with its network of iTunes customers. These corporations all leverage their networks. As a result, they achieve something far more powerful than what each entity could do on its own.

The same applies to you. With your network, you can accomplish things quicker, more efficiently, and more effectively and you can go farther than you can do so alone. More heads are definitely better than one.

Now here's the most important thing to remember about networking: Don't go into networking counting and anticipating all the advantages or benefits you will gain from each connection. Instead, focus on how you can be of service to those people or how you can help them achieve their goals. Your rewards (including the intangible goodwill and shared learning) will come naturally, organically, later or when you least expect them. Interestingly, those who don't think of their own personal gain seem to always end up getting the most from networking. Isn't that ironic?

In this chapter, we cover various aspects of networking, including the patience required to develop and nurture relationships, the kind of people you should add to your network, and the strategies for introverts and for networking up.

NETWORKING DONE RIGHT

Networking is not about collecting business cards at cocktail receptions or taking new contacts out for lunch or coffee and then forgetting all about them until you have to ask a favor or a question and then disappearing from their life again until you need something—and then rinse, repeat. That's the surest way to make them feel used and thus to disassociate from you altogether. They might do as you requested the first time (perhaps to be nice), but you won't hear from them again the next time you come calling.

So what should you do to get this right? Following are some of our suggestions. These practices might seem like common sense, but they are rarely commonly practiced. Do them without fail throughout your career, and you will create a network so rich and robust that it can lead to and sustain your career success.

Develop and Maintain Lasting Relationships

Treat networking as a lifestyle, something you do regularly as a habit, not as some one-time effort. Send notes and cards to thank them for spending time with you recently. Make phone calls to check in. E-mail a link to an article that you know they are interested in (professionally or personally). Meet them when you're in their town (or vice versa) or when you're both at a social or professional event. Like, comment on, or share their social media posts. Support their initiatives. Extend an offer to help before they ask or even if they don't ask. Get to know them personally (respecting their boundaries, of course), and remember some details about them that you can bring up the next time you see each other again. Introduce them to others you think they may be interested in getting to know.

These little acts add up and help you build a lasting relationship with every member of your network. They show you care about them and your connection. They show your strength of character. They show you are there to serve their needs and interests, not the other way around.

Because of the rapport you're establishing, one day in the future you may feel less awkward or uncomfortable about, for example, approaching a CEO contact for a job recommendation or asking a colleague for information that is not readily accessible (like if a coveted position is soon to open up because of unforeseen staffing changes).

Be Patient

Networking is a lot of things, but fast it is not. No instant gratification here. But that's to be expected. After all, no one can build a lasting relationship in a few hours, weeks, or even months. If you want to do networking right, you have to invest time into it (read: years, even decades), and you have to practice patience. This means you have to continually meet people, earn their trust and respect, get to know them, pay attention to their needs, and serve them or make them look good—all without expecting anything in return. Again, network when you don't need to network (just like you should look for a job when you don't need a job). This network will be there for you to draw from when you do need it for whatever reason—big or small—and through seasons of your life when it is not your top priority.

If you don't put in the time and patience, you may be creating superficial, short-term connections in which everyone involved is just in it to use everyone else and then burn all bridges. This should go without saying, but burning bridges is never, ever a good move. Healthcare is a small world. You never know where you could end up later in your career. The people you offend, take advantage of, mistreat, or abandon today could be the very same people you could be working for or could be offering that next golden opportunity tomorrow.

Diversify Your Network

Get connected with stellar people inside and outside your industry and area of expertise. For example, you could network with clinicians, academics and educators, business leaders, consumer advocates, healthcare quality researchers, health policymakers, and patient groups. Plus, you could network with the following:

- Your mentors
- Rising stars and centers of influence in your organization
- Thought leaders in your industry and other related industries (e.g., pharmaceutical, long-term care)
- Former colleagues
- Former professors and classmates as well as alumni from your undergraduate and graduate programs

- Peers and emerging leaders in your community or industry
- Staff of your professional associations
- Representatives from your civic and charitable organizations (e.g., nonprofits, faith-based groups, PTA, chambers of commerce, and rotary clubs)

The point here is to surround yourself with a good mix of people—in terms of gender, age or generation, geography, industry, education and training, ethnicity or cultural background, and so on. Fostering a diverse network exposes you to various styles, walks of life, perspectives, areas of expertise, and bodies of knowledge that help cultivate your well-roundedness and open-mindedness. This way, you are not isolated from other disciplines and your influence extends beyond your field.

Be Selective

Speaking of influence, remember in Chapter 6 we discussed what we called the *average five* theory? This is the idea that the five people you spend the most time with shape and influence you, and you in turn shape and influence five more people and on the cycle goes. Because of this influence, you and those closest to you share the same beliefs, mentality, and even hobbies or interests. They also reflect, in general, your health, financial, and career status.

The professionals in your network exert the same kind of influence on you, so be cautious when selecting your associates. Pick people who are like-minded and can reinforce or support your growth (and vice versa). Stay away from those who are negative and whose career choices or reputation could hurt yours. Serving them could prove challenging.

Be Consistent

Consistency is key in good leadership and in good networking. Think about your favorite supervisor or manager. Chances are she or he gives you feedback—both positive and negative—on a regular basis and not just when something goes wrong or during your annual evaluation. The manager is consistent and methodical with giving you input and asking you to make adjustments when needed. This way, you always know not only how you're performing your duties but also where you stand with the manager and what is expected of you. Best of all, you get no surprises.

Networking should be treated with the same consistent strategy. Not only should you keep engaging with the people in your network (and doing so selflessly), but you should also keep seizing new opportunities to network (see Exhibit 9.2). Otherwise, one day you might be shocked to find that the network you've built over many years has diminished in both strength and number.

Last but not least: Make sure your offline (or "real-life" self) and online personas are consistent with each other. Be authentic or be your true self regardless of whether you're interacting with your network on social media or face to face. Displaying two different personalities or pretending you're more or other than who you are will confuse your audience and make them think you are playing games at best and are untrustworthy at worst.

Exhibit 9.2 Seven Strategies for Growing Your Network

Valuable resources are all around you, and with just a little bit of legwork you can easily tap into them. Take the initiative to seek out new networking relationships whenever you can. Here are just a few ways:

1. *Work the alumni network.* Whether you are still a student, just graduated, or finished your degree decades ago, you can check out your college's/university's rich catalogue of alumni. Most schools keep good tabs on their high-performing former students and would be able to connect you with them. From this catalogue, you can find a

(continued)

potential mentor or a networking partner in your geographic area or area of interest.

2. *Launch an internal search.* Identify those in your organization who have political capital and reach out to them. These individuals may be up-and-coming leaders or colleagues who may be a step or two ahead of you career-wise. Whatever the case is, asking them separately to join you for a 30-minute coffee break or a 1-hour lunch conversation can go a long way.

3. *Get involved in your community.* Choose a local cause that is near and dear to your heart—anything from a grassroots movement to a young professionals civic group to a nonprofit organization. Call and ask how you can volunteer. This enables you to stay informed about the issues in your community, serve other people, hone skills that you may not use on a daily basis, develop personally, and meet people and build relationships. Volunteering will give more to you than you give to it. That's a fact.

   Healthcare leadership volunteering is also possible. For example, Laurie's mentor encouraged her to sit on the board of her local ACHE chapter in Nebraska. She was only two years into her career, so she thought, "What could I possibly have to offer?" Her volunteer service meant doing event planning, contact management, hosting speakers, and various other grunt work. Not glamorous, but very personally and professionally rewarding. It afforded her a fantastic opportunity to connect with many influential healthcare leaders in the area.

4. *Become a card-carrying member of professional associations.* Industry organizations give you opportunities to meet local and national healthcare leaders, to share and learn best practices in various areas of healthcare management, and to lead or participate in discussions about industry issues, among other benefits. Plus, you get to connect with like-minded professionals who are on a similar career path or season of life as you. Reach out to the local chapter of these associations. Their representatives can help you get started. (See Exhibit 9.3 for more discussion on association membership.)

5. *Take advantage of social media and other online resources.* If you're not yet *professionally* active online, start. Now. This goes beyond having a passive account on LinkedIn, Twitter, Facebook, and other social media platforms. This involves active engagement, including following trusted thought leaders, movers and shakers, pioneers and innovators, and organizational leaders; sharing industry-related news, research and case studies, journal articles, and other informative tidbits with your connections; writing (long or short)

(continued)

healthcare-related posts that stimulate dialogue between you and readers; and hosting or participating in virtual discussions about topics that affect the industry. Doing so can quickly build up your professional online presence, and pretty soon it will lead to new contacts that you can nurture into networking relationships.

6. *Introduce yourself.* At events, step out of your comfort zone. Don't default to sitting with your friends or existing contacts for the whole day. That doesn't do you or them any favor. Catch up with them before or after (or whatever works for you), but excuse yourself during the event so that you (and they) can meet and mingle with other attendees, session presenters, lead speakers, exhibitors (these are not just vendors but representatives of organizations), and so on. Arrive early or stay late to maximize your time, if you must. Introducing yourself to strangers may be uncomfortable and nerve-wracking, but remember that just about everyone there is in the same situation as you and is feeling the same thing. And we assure you that the vast majority of people at these events are pleasant and receptive to networking with you.

Let's go back to introducing yourself to the speaker. Before the speaker's presentation, approach him or her; you could *briefly* talk about who you are and why you're looking forward to the talk, and you could ask whether you could contact him or her in the future should you have any follow-up questions or if you could be of service. By doing this, you're making your presence known to a well-respected and influential person (otherwise he or she wouldn't be presenting in the first place!) and you're opening lines of communication between the two of you (which could lead to a mentorship or networking relationship). The speaker may reference you as an example during the presentation, which would be a bonus as that will increase your visibility and help you make more connections during the event.

7. *Help others build their network.* If you're consistent enough to have developed a robust network, take the initiative to introduce pairs of people you know to each other, if you think they would be good partners and would gain mutual benefits. Call it network matchmaking. For example, do you know a professor looking desperately for a research assistant? Do you know a student or a new careerist aspiring to be in academia? Voilà, you got a match! Go and introduce them to each other. These pairings may not always work, but the point is you're exercising the value of your network and making that network valuable for others as well. And the more you help others, the better your reputation gets and the more connections come your way and the more you can help and so on. Good begets good; don't forget that.

Exhibit 9.3 Association Membership

Six years ago, the William E. Smith Institute for Association Research published the findings of a study on association membership. The report revealed that association members earn more, like their jobs more, and are even happier than people who do not belong to any association (Brooks 2008). Because the research was done for the association community, these results are likely biased, so take them with a grain of salt. That being said, our personal experience and recommendation align with this research.

But do note: Simply being a member and paying your annual dues will not lead to the well-connected career you want, just as merely having a gym membership will not lead to the strong body you want. You have to take advantage of the resources and privileges available to you. You have to actively engage to get as much value out of that association as you can.

Following is a short list (certainly not all-inclusive) of healthcare associations we suggest you look into:

- American College of Healthcare Executives (ACHE)
- American Health Care Association (AHCA)
- American Hospital Association (AHA)
- Asian Health Care Leaders Association (AHCLA)
- Healthcare Financial Management Association (HFMA)
- Healthcare Information and Management Systems Society (HIMSS)
- Medical Group Management Association (MGMA)
- National Association of Health Services Executives (NAHSE)
- National Forum for Latino Healthcare Executives (NFLHE)
- Specialization associations (e.g., American Association of Orthopaedic Executives, American Academy of Ophthalmic Executives, Association for Directors of Radiation Oncology Programs)

Plus, you can check out Young Professional (YP) groups in your community as well as local or industry leadership programs (e.g., Leadership Omaha).

Present Yourself as a Memorable and Genuine Professional

Your personal and professional selves (the things you can change and manage) combined with your reputation (the things others say about you that you cannot control) make up your personal brand (see Chapter 5). The *you* brand is what others see when you network. You must present it in a memorable and genuine fashion. Here are some tips on how you can set yourself apart among your contacts:

- *Dress and conduct yourself* as if *you are already holding the position you desire.* Always be aware of the nature and location of the networking event and dress appropriately. If the setting is casual, be on the sharper edge of business casual. You won't find too many healthcare CEOs, for example, in jeans and a fleece or in ill-fitted khakis and a golf shirt. If you're unsure, find out the dress code.

  Don't be memorable for the wrong reasons. Be remembered as the one person who wore a tailored suit, not as the one who drank too much at the reception and spoke too loudly and told inappropriate jokes. Regardless of how casual the networking event is, it isn't permission to behave unprofessionally or to forget all the rules of social decorum. You are there to spark new professional relationships and invest in existing ones. You are not there to draw negative attention to yourself or be the "life of the party" so to speak; that behavior may only garner you an embarrassing mention in someone's blog, tweet, Facebook post, or LinkedIn update—or worse, a red flag in the memory of a key center of influence.

  Be polite, willing to participate in activities, friendly, and approachable. You don't have to be perky, but you should be positive (not sarcastic, cynical, or a contrarian). You don't have to be the most intelligent person in the room or to know everything, but you should be able to hold a conversation about a host of topics (including healthcare trends) with a diverse group. And you don't have to be the best talker, but you should be an active listener; this entails not just nodding your head but also asking follow-up questions and occasionally relating to what is being said.

- *Be a genuine connector.* Introducing your associates to those you believe they ought to know and then getting out of their way is one of the surest ways to show that you're genuine about serving others, that you're not in the relationship just to benefit you, and that you're looking out for their interests. If you're only pretending to care, your contacts will see right through it. For example, if you strongly urge a current colleague to interview with a hiring manager you know from another organization in the guise of "helping" the coworker practice her interviewing skills, but in reality this is your own plot to push her out because you secretly want her position, then your behavior and intentions are purely selfish. When (not if) your colleague finds out what you're doing, she could hurt your reputation. And thanks to the Internet, word travels fast. It takes a long time to rebuild your brand from this kind of offense.

- *Stay informed, and be thoughtful.* On top of sending handwritten notes for various purposes (e.g., saying thanks, congratulations, or just a hello), you should keep yourself updated on what your associates are doing. Set up Google alerts for the leading organizations and individuals in your network. Check your connections' LinkedIn updates. Read association newsletters and trade magazines. Did anyone publish an article, switch jobs or get promoted, win an award or a notable honor, earn a certification, pass an exam, launch a business or a product, or participate in a successful initiative? Use this knowledge to reach out and make a warm contact. How would you feel if someone you once connected with, but hadn't touched based with in a while, sent you a surprise e-mail congratulating you on a recent promotion? It would be a memorable moment, that's for sure. And all it took was a minute of their time.

Staying informed can also help you leave a great impression—and that's a plus for a new careerist. For example, when your CEO asks if anyone is aware of a proposed hospital legislation in a neighboring state and its potential implication for your organization, you're going to want to know exactly what the CEO's talking about and you're going to want to be able to share your opinion.

Finally, remember the things that are important to your contacts, and bring them up in your conversation. How are your twin three-year-old granddaughters? Are you still volunteering at the women's shelter? Have you finished building that boat with your son? Teddy Roosevelt's quote, "People don't care how much you know, until they know how much you care," rings true here.

NETWORKING FOR INTROVERTS

The best networkers are extroverts, right? We beg to differ.

We believe that being self-aware and being consistent at networking trump differences in personality. You don't have to be gregarious or a social butterfly, flitting from one group to the next, to attract contacts. You can be shy or reserved and still be able to build lasting networking relationships. The key is to know how you operate. Do you prefer e-mails and notes to phone calls and face to face? Are you more comfortable with one-on-one than with group activity? Does the idea of entering a circle of strangers to introduce yourself terrify you? Once you understand these and other things about yourself, you can develop your own networking approach. Although the recommendations we present in this chapter offer something for both introverts and extroverts, we urge you to create an approach that works best for you. (Note that the advice we give here may apply to everybody, not just introverts.)

Whatever you do, don't skip networking events just because you don't think you could handle them. Go! Show up! Practice introducing yourself in the mirror, over and over and over until you become masterful (or at least proficient) at it. Work on your elevator speech—that is, what you'd like to say about yourself—and questions you'd like to ask when you meet someone new. Don't approach crowds, if you're uncomfortable; strike up a conversation with an individual and then move on to another. Don't forget to exchange business cards, as you'll want to follow-up later to thank the person for the chat or to fill in the blanks that you might have forgotten in your nervous state. And if you write well, wow your new contacts with a sincere note; you could make a good impression that way, if you thought you didn't during your initial meeting.

Social media can also help. Before the event, reach out to a few of your contacts via LinkedIn, Twitter, or Facebook. Prime the pump, so to speak. Let them know you're looking forward to finally meeting face to face. This will make the meeting much more comfortable, efficient, and effective.

Networking is not a talent or a character trait. It's a skill you can learn that doesn't require you to become someone you're not. All it needs is your consistent input.

NETWORK UP

Heard of the term "marry up"? Now let's introduce you to the concept of *network up*. By this we mean keep company with the big boys and girls, the wise, the real deals. Soon enough, you'll become the company you keep.

We're not talking about hanging out with chief executives or senior-level managers here (although you should approach them as well). We're talking about surrounding yourself with high performers and high achievers (no matter their organizational titles or rank). These are people who have a strong work ethic, who are ambitious and driven, who are disciplined and tenacious, who make things happen, who try even at the risk of failure and embarrassment, and who bring their A game all the time—and insist you do, too. A network filled with these types of people may be intimidating initially because they can be demanding and make your nerves dance a little bit, but they will inspire you to be better at everything you do.

Face it: Being the best of the bottom of the barrel is not a compliment. It might make others view you as a slacker by association. And that's a toxic perception, especially when you're just starting out and trying to prove yourself. So, as we said earlier, select your associates carefully.

It's natural for you to think you're not good enough, at this early stage, to associate with the movers and shakers, but snap out of it! Stretch yourself, and don't let any naysayers stop you. You'll steadily gain confidence once you realize that these people are receptive to you. That's the first step. The second step is to seek out these high achievers and connect with them. Look around your department, organization, community, and industry to identify those whose character, style, skills, and knowledge impress you. The rest of the steps are all up to you.

Five Benefits of Networking Up

1. *Learning opportunity.* When you fill your sphere of influence with wise professionals, you will inevitably learn something—from their successes, mistakes or failures, experiences, and daily habits. It's up to you to observe, listen for, and absorb the lessons. The reverse is true, too. If you find that your network comprises people who are comfortable with the status quo and the mediocre and who don't care whether you succeed or fail, then you'll learn those negative habits.

2. *Better accountability.* When you network up, you are also signing yourself up to be accountable for whatever goals you set for yourself. These people are driven to achieve, so they expect the same from you. All of a sudden, you've got a network of people holding you responsible for your own good. They will check on your progress, motivate and encourage you, shoot down every one of your excuses, give you advice and tools (even tough love), help you put things in perspective when you're faced with big decisions and barriers or if you fall short, and then challenge you to try again and again. With this kind of support, you'll have no excuse to give up or to not take your own growth seriously.

3. *Source of inspiration.* Even though the associates that you admire and want to emulate are not perfect, they are inspirational to you anyway. If you spend enough time with them, you'll find yourself doing what they do, doing what they ask or imply, and doing the right thing. That's what happens in general when you connect with people you see as role models and as guides or teachers. Their actions, experiences, accomplishments, and wisdom compel you to follow their lead and to strive to be as good.

4. *Reason to stretch yourself.* Networking up may feel like you're in a secret competition with your connections. This motivates you to step up your game to catch up with, keep up with, or outpace their moves. This healthy challenge is a good thing, even fun! The more you stretch yourself, the better you get (even if you fail). And the better you get, the more opportunities (networking or otherwise) come your way. And the more opportunities come your way, the closer you get to your goals.

5. *Exercise in humility.* Amid all these high performers, inspiration, and competitors, it's impossible not to feel humbled. After all, you're surrounded by people who have stellar brands and whose reputation precedes them. Humility works two ways here. First, you're humbled by the caliber of the people around you. Second, you're humbled by the fact that you have a lot more growing up and learning to do, by your network's generosity in mentoring or teaching you—regardless of whether they do it deliberately or unintentionally, and by the lack of self-awareness and abundance of ego you've displayed in the past when you thought you had already arrived.

Board of Career Advisors

From your network of high performers, you can select the members of what we call a *board of career advisors* (aka sphere of influence, which is discussed in earlier chapters). These are people you trust to keep your confidences, to serve as a sounding board for your ideas and concerns, to give you honest feedback, and to advise you on various professional matters. They don't necessarily have to be friends, but they could include acquaintances, friends, and even family members. Most important, they must exercise discretion (as you will). This is a must, not an option.

Embrace your board of career advisors, and serve its members with tender, loving care. But remember to be careful about what and how much you divulge. There is no place for TMI (too much information) in leadership, although it may be tempting to let your guard down once you get closer to certain members of your board. It's a delicate balance you have to strike, we know. On the one hand, you want to be authentic and share everything (including organizational information few people have access to), but on the other hand, you have a responsibility to keep things professional and at arm's length. If you assemble a board of trustworthy, mature people, though, you can rest assured they will understand where you're coming from. (This board concept is discussed more in Chapter 10.)

NETWORKING ACCORDING TO YOUR SEASON OF LIFE

Your networking approach and needs will differ depending on the season of your life. At the beginning of your career, perhaps without the obligations of a spouse or young children, investing heavily in your networking efforts may come easily. But as your seasons change (for example, when you get married, raise a family, take on more responsibilities at work), your ability to attend evening networking events, weekend community volunteer activities, or leadership or association engagements may become limited. These obligations and commitments could force you to be more strategic in how you invest in networking.

That's totally okay. Normal and expected, even. Embrace the seasons of your life and network accordingly. Just don't stop networking entirely. No matter how much or how little time you dedicate to networking, be intentional about what you choose to participate in.

Evaluate your goals and objectives every once in a while to see if your time is being invested in a manner that nets a productive outcome. Consider what you commit to and what you don't. Every "yes" you say means a "no" to something else. Make it clear to those you say "no" to that it simply means "not now" and not forever.

The lesson here is to network consistently and as much as you can early in your career, before family and other obligations become your highest priorities. Again, this is a tiny act with a compounding effect. That is, every "deposit" you make into your networking bank adds up. First, it establishes a positive habit. And later, when you are less able to network as much, you can "withdraw" from this bank, allowing you to still take advantage of your earlier efforts.

Remember These

- With your network, you can accomplish things quicker, more efficiently, and more effectively and you can go farther than you can do so alone.
- Don't go into networking counting and anticipating all the advantages or benefits you will gain from each connection. Instead, focus on how you can be of service to those people or how you can help them achieve their goals.
- Treat networking as a lifestyle, something you do regularly as a habit, not as some one-time effort.
- If you want to do networking right, you have to invest time into it (read: years, even decades).
- Fostering a diverse network exposes you to various styles, walks of life, perspectives, areas of expertise, and bodies of knowledge that help cultivate your well-roundedness and open-mindedness.
- The professionals in your network exert the same kind of influence on you, so be cautious when selecting your

$\rightarrow$

---

associates. Pick people who are like-minded and can reinforce or support your growth (and vice versa).

- Not only should you keep engaging with the people in your network (and doing so selflessly), but you should also keep seizing new opportunities to network.

- Being self-aware and being consistent at networking trump differences in personality. You don't have to be gregarious or a social butterfly to attract contacts. You can be shy or reserved and still be able to build lasting networking relationships.

- Network up: Surround yourself with high performers and high achievers. Soon enough, you'll become the company you keep.

- Your networking approach and needs will differ depending on the season of your life. No matter how much or how little time you dedicate to networking, be intentional about what you choose to participate in.

REFERENCE

Brooks, A. C. 2008. *Where Winners Meet: Why Happier, More Successful People Gravitate Toward Associations.* Accessed August 2014. www.nacva.com/pdf /SmithInst_winners.pdf.

Note to My 25-Year-Old Self

At age 25, newly married and serving as an administrative dietitian responsible for a 500-bed hospital kitchen, I knew I needed to complete postgraduate work to advance my career. Little did I know then that my educational journey would lead me beyond dietetics and into healthcare leadership. Working full-time and taking healthcare administration classes on a part-time basis opened my eyes, both academically and practically. I had opportunities to network internally and become involved in hospitalwide committees. By age 30, I had transitioned into hospital administration.

A guiding principle early on should be network or no work. Understand the value of connections—in the workplace, in the local community, and in the industry. Your network will serve as the foundation for your career and will be a resource to draw on—from securing a fellowship to job advancement to industry leadership appointment. Developing a strong network of connections does not just happen; it is an investment that needs to be cultivated and maintained.

Take strategic risks. Be creative, and try new things. Accept new challenges, and do not be afraid of change. Never stop learning, and keep adding to your toolbox of job skills. It is so much better to accept roles that interest you or that are aligned with your career goals than to be "volunteered" and then find yourself in a direction you would not have chosen. Do not be afraid to stretch yourself and show others your capabilities. Do your best to stay positive, even if you find yourself busy making lemonade out of the lemons coming your way.

Few people work alone so when you are building your team, surround yourself with strong people. Choose individuals who complement your strengths and weaknesses and who share your values; you will learn from them, and they will challenge you to perform at your highest potential. Together, you will form a strong successful team that will outperform anything you could do alone.

Take time to give back to the profession and the community. Mentor or coach others either in your own organization or beyond. Visit student groups or provide shadowing experiences to encourage those entering or advancing in the field. Serve on community committees/boards that interest you and that will benefit from your presence. You will gain new knowledge from those experiences, which will be useful in your career, and you will be enriched by the opportunity to serve.

Never forget the Golden Rule while traveling along your professional path. Your professional reputation and personal brand will thank you.

Lastly, seek out mentors and coaches. Their insights will be invaluable to your success. Take every opportunity to learn from those who have been there and whose wisdom will equip you to grapple with the challenges of leadership.

Remember to take time for yourself and your family. Your organization and your home team will be better off with a happy, healthy person at the helm.

May you do great things—and have some fun along the way as well!

Signed,
Deborah Y. Rasper, LFACHE
Governor (2006–2009), American College of Healthcare Executives
Retired Administrator, St. Vincent Mercy Hospital

CHAPTER 10

Engage a Mentor, Be a Mentor

"If I hadn't had mentors, I wouldn't be here today. I'm a
product of great mentoring, great coaching. . . . Coaches or
mentors are very important. They could be anyone—your
husband, other family members, or your boss."

—*Indra Nooyi, CEO, PepsiCo*

Reading Points

- Identifying a Mentor

- Putting Together a Board of Career Advisors

- Getting Started

- Giving Back to the Field

WHAT COMES TO mind when you think of a mentor? Chances
are you envision someone a couple of decades older than you,
someone with a senior leadership title or in a position of power, or
someone well known in the community. But, in reality, a mentor
is not as out of reach as you may imagine. She or he can come from
all walks of life and is likely already playing an important role in
your life or career; it could even be you—to someone else, that is.

Although no definitive guideline exists for who a mentor should be or what a mentoring relationship should entail, there is a clear and known characteristic shared by all mentors: They enrich your life by contributing to your personal growth and/or professional development. How do they do this? By serving as your teacher, role model, sounding board, cheerleader, support system, devil's advocate, helping hand, confidante, and so on.

Specifically, mentors can

- *help you realize your full potential.* This is really at the heart of mentoring. Mentors see the potential in you, and they do what they can to nudge (even push) you toward becoming the person or professional you could be. They point you to resources for developing your natural abilities and aptitudes.

- *set an example.* Experienced professionals carry a hefty toolkit full of tools (e.g., advice, methods, strategies, tactics, solutions) they have picked up throughout their career. As mentors, they willingly share these tools and stories of their mistakes. The goal is to make their experiences into examples so that you can avoid the same mistakes they committed and guide you out of the wrong path.

- *provide honest feedback.* As an early careerist, you need to surround yourself with individuals who don't soothe and coddle your ego all the time and thus are not afraid to "tell it like it is." Such a mentor understands that a candid critique will strengthen your character, skills, and performance better than nonstop praise (which may not always be genuine) and agreement can ever do.

- *extend opportunities.* Experienced mentors, by virtue of the professional clout they've amassed over the years, may be in a position to leverage their contacts and reputation for your benefit. This opens career doors for you to walk or run through.

- *help you understand yourself better.* Great mentors ask questions. Then, they listen for the answers and probe with follow-up questions. By doing so, they help you become more self-aware, which is a foundation for your success.
- *challenge your status quo.* Mentors push you out of your comfort zone by presenting perspectives you hadn't considered before, challenging you to stretch yourself, assuring you that it's ok to fail and make mistakes, and encouraging you to try something new.

In this chapter, we walk you through the basics of mentorship. We cover the hows of identifying a mentor and assembling a board of career advisors, the whys of serving your board and mentor, and the when of giving back to the field.

IDENTIFYING A MENTOR

Visualize the position you'd like to fill, the kind of person and leader you'd like to be, and the influence you'd like to have on others in the future. Observe people who today are in the exact place that you want to be in tomorrow. Note what they do and why, how they interact with and serve others, what skills and experiences they have, what their reputation is among others, who their mentors are and who makes up their network or sphere of influence, how self-aware they are, what career path they took (or are taking) to reach their ultimate goals, whether they're continual learners and willing teachers (especially to up-and-comers), and so on. If you like what you see, then you can approach one or two of those people to be your mentor (you don't have to limit yourself to one).

Don't be afraid to ask a CEO or senior executive. They were in your shoes once, so they'll be able to relate to your early career experiences and mentoring needs. But don't limit your search for a mentor in the C-suite, either. Look around you and explore other avenues, if your regular network does not connect you to a mentor. Here are our recommendations:

1. Turn to your alumni network for slightly older peers—those only two or three years ahead of you—who are still amid their early-career struggles or challenges and thus can offer you timely and relevant insights and guidance.

2. Scan your organization for the rising stars (e.g., young managers, project leads, mid-level employees)—those whose name you often hear and who have earned the trust, respect, and admiration of the internal and external people they've worked with. The excellent job they do and their reputation expose them to diverse experiences, opportunities, people, approaches, and challenges. You can learn a lot from them.

3. Join a professional or charitable board in your community, or volunteer for a local cause you support. There, you'll find a mix of individuals from whom you can glean out-of-industry perspectives and advice that are applicable to your life and work.

4. Serve your boss and profession. Both are enormous resources. Your boss is already serving as your daily teacher, and if you make her or him look good (by being the reliable go-to person), you will learn even more. Association membership and their events are mentorship (not just networking) mines. The more you develop yourself professionally, the more visibility you gain in the field and the better your chances of attracting the mentors that suit you.

The Authenticity Factor

Authenticity is a big factor in an effective mentoring relationship. As a mentee, you can't expect to get helpful advice and guidance from your mentor if you aren't honest about yourself and your concerns, worries, goals, and dreams. Your mentor will find it hard to get through to you if you are pretending to be someone you're not. Be open about your faults and shortcomings, and accept responsibility for fixing or improving them. Allow yourself to be groomed, to be taught, to be criticized, and to be challenged. Embrace your role as the student, and absorb as much as you can.

Choose a mentor who is also willing to be genuine, honest, and open with you. Mutual sharing of triumphs is great, but mutual sharing of defeats is a must. After all, stories about failures, embarrassment, or disappointments resonate louder than stories about wins and accomplishments. The latter type may be more inspiring, but the former type (although may be difficult to tell) is more real, relatable, humbling, and educational. It reminds us no one's career path is perfect, and it encourages us to keep trying despite the mistakes and conflicts that are always just waiting to happen. Failed experiences are what usually stick in the mind. After all, everyone has experienced a low point but not everyone has experienced success.

PUTTING TOGETHER A BOARD OF CAREER ADVISORS

As we discussed in Chapter 9, a board of career advisors is made up of people who serve many purposes and fill many roles, like mentor, advocate or champion, confidante, role model, and even critic. Members of this board may include colleagues and other acquaintances, members of your professional network, family, and friends. You could meet with each in person, by phone, or online on a regular (daily, weekly, monthly, quarterly) or sporadic basis.

Your board gives you diverse perspectives as well as access to resources and information that you can't get anywhere else. (We're not talking about sharing organizational secrets here; remember, true professionals practice discretion and divulge no confidential or irrelevant work-related information.) This way, it is a huge contributor to your personal and professional growth.

When assembling your own board, think of the individuals who come to mind when you ask these questions:

- Who has encouraged my professional development and made me a better leader?
- Who has contributed to my success by guiding and/or advising me?
- Who has challenged me and holds me to my goals?
- Who sees my potential?
- Whom do I admire?
- Whose leadership style (e.g., servant leadership, character-driven leadership) would I like to emulate?
- Who has a strong reputation or personal brand in the industry or community?

Plus, don't overlook your "competitors" or those who are pursuing the same things you're after. Add them to your board as well. They're competition *not* in the true sense of that word (because really you're competing with only yourself and running your career path at your own pace; as we've said in an earlier chapter, you shouldn't compare yourself to others) but in the context of having someone challenge you to get in the game in the first place, to set your bar higher, to hold yourself accountable for the results.

Most important, just like in networking, always consider how you can serve the members of this board and maintain a relationship and rapport with each of them. Popping up in their lives every once in a while and only when you need a favor is never, ever advisable. Make a true effort in this regard.

In case you're wondering what a board of advisors looks like, here's a peek into our own. We wrote our respective list in first person to give you a flavor of what each member on our board truly means to us.

Laurie's board:

- The pragmatist: Wes, my husband, keeps me grounded when I want to fly away. When I make an assumption, he challenges it with realistic considerations. When I want to jump, he asks me to be more deliberate and weigh the risks.
- The perspective: Natalie, my peer and co-author, gets me and has invaluable insight into the challenges and circumstances that I face professionally. She understands where I've been and where I'm going, and she inspires me to push harder.
- The cheerleader: Mike always encourages me no matter what. He believes in me and picks me up by the scruff when I feel broken or when I fall down.
- The professional: Steph is an executive who is more seasoned than I career-wise. She is the embodiment of professional development. She has the background (she's "been there" after all) and is very honest and forthcoming about her experiences to help me not only identify any issues or missteps but also reinforce and validate my goals.
- The wise one: Dean is my Yoda, for you *Star Wars* buffs out there. This physician, a long-time client and now friend, is the calm, level-headed voice of reason even amid the most challenging and chaotic of circumstances. He is rational and thorough, patient and composed. His perspective is priceless.
- The catalyst: Eric drives me to be better in my work. If ever I'm inclined to coast, he compels me to push harder. Over the years, we've established a rhythm, spurring

strong growth in each other and consistently raising the bar for each other.

- The character builder: Bob is my first mentor. He was very influential and guided me during the early stages of my career. Now, more than a decade later, he continues to be my compass. He demonstrated (and, in turn, shaped in me) those intangibles a leader simply can't put a price on, like integrity and character. His example has had a deep and lasting impact on me.

Natalie's board:

- Rory, my husband, perpetually challenges me and pushes me to learn something new, do something different, demand more from myself, and stretch myself in such a way that I'm always a little uncomfortable and never complacent. As the CEO of his own company, he understands what I do as a CEO. And, because he is not in healthcare, he offers me perspectives and insights that I don't typically encounter in the industry but have deeply enhanced my own strategies.

- Rulon, my fellowship preceptor and later my first healthcare boss, is not only a mentor but also a friend. Because we have known each other since the beginning of my career, I can rely on him to give me well-rounded or global advice that takes into account not just my professional needs and goals but also those of my family and my personal interests. Plus, he is so knowledgeable about the industry that saying he's a great resource is a huge understatement. To put it simply, this man taught me how to be a CEO and to this day continues to inspire me to be the caliber of leader he is. If I'm even half as kind and half as good as he is, I'd consider myself a success.

- Kevin, my mentor and supporter, has been opening his door for me since the first day we met. Not only does he regularly check on my career progress, but he also holds me accountable for the goals I've set for myself. He never hesitates to ask me the tough questions, does not sugarcoat his opinions, and offers constructive critique of my professional decisions and actions. He's one of the most generous and character-driven people I know, freely giving his time, attention, compassion, and expertise to serve others.

- Laurie, my coauthor and session cofacilitator, needs no introduction. Just as a competitive runner runs better when racing fast runners, I'm encouraged to rise to the occasion and give only my best performance when I'm around such a high achiever and hard worker like Laurie. She and I occupy the same space in our careers, and we each relate to the other's experiences.

- Robb, a colleague and a tireless advocate, is my go-to person for the day-to-day operational issues I encounter in my role. If I'm navigating politically delicate waters, for example, I call him for his advice and input—and he never steers me wrong. The wealth of information, intelligence, lessons, and instincts he eagerly shares with those around him is second only to the warmth, humility, and openness he displays. He is a true servant leader and is a calm and reassuring presence in my life.

- Sheila, a former colleague but a forever friend, is my kindred spirit and cheerleader. She re-energizes me when I'm feeling dejected and overwhelmed, and she doesn't judge me for my shortcomings. She reminds me why I do what I do and why I love it. And she's genuinely happy for my accomplishments and genuinely cares about my well-being—in and out of the office. We share a bond that transcends job titles, backgrounds, experiences, physical distance, and everything else.

GETTING STARTED

The first time you meet with a potential mentor, focus on simply having a conversation. Introduce/reintroduce yourself, ask about the person's role and responsibilities, ask follow-up questions about what the person brings up, and listen and watch intently (you can learn a lot about someone just by listening and watching). If personal details enter the discussion, allow them. They're a natural part of a dialogue. Don't (or try not to) ask for a mentoring relationship right out of the gate. After all, you still have to assess whether the person's career path, experience, style, character, and reputation are a good fit with yours (and vice versa). If the initial meeting doesn't turn out to be a mentoring relationship, then at least you've gained another professional to add to your network.

The meeting itself doesn't have to be face to face, which is difficult to do if you're in two different cities or states. You could talk on the phone or perhaps through Skype. For a high-profile mentor (like a large system CEO), often you would have to schedule a time to talk or have lunch or dinner, not just pick up the phone to make casual plans.

Serving the Mentor

At the start of (or even before) a new mentoring relationship, you may be plagued with feelings of intimidation, inadequacy, and self-doubt. You may wonder, "What do I have to offer this person?" And you're right on track when you worry about this, because it means you understand the give-and-take nature of mentorship.

Let's repeat what we've said before: You *do* have something to offer. Much of a mentoring relationship is the imparting of wisdom by the mentor to the mentee. But the mentee doesn't come to this union empty handed. Exhibit 10.1 breaks down the contributions of a mentee.

Exhibit 10.1: What a Mentee Can Offer to a Mentor

- *Time.* A hospital CEO has precious little time, but you—at this stage in your career—should spare some time and be flexible. Be selfless. When making an appointment with your mentor, accommodate his or her schedule (even if it's after work hours). Show up or call on time and prepare for the meeting, gathering all your questions, concerns, and updates beforehand to make the meeting as productive as possible. And don't go over the time allotted (or worse, monopolize the entire conversation with sporadic questions) because, more often than not, your mentor must get back to a pressing task or project. The point here is not only to maximize the time carved out for you but also to be respectful of your mentor's other commitments. Sometimes you may be of help by simply listening to your mentor. Tune into that and identify any areas where you can help out.

- *Connections.* You may think your professional circle pales in comparison to that of your seasoned mentor (and in most every way, it probably does). However, in some ways your circle may be bigger than that of your mentor because you're likely more social media savvy. You could help your mentor enlarge or strengthen this network by introducing him or her to online forums and other resources.

- *Resources.* Combined, your time flexibility, Internet savvy, and networking skills put you in a position to solve a problem that your mentor may be grappling with. You could offer to do some online and offline research, to consult with your board of career advisors or peers, or to review proposals or other documents. In this way, your mentor sees you as an extension, another pair of eyes and hands that can help when needed.

- *Expertise.* What's your sweet spot? Are you an expert in a certain area (like coding, blogging, or marketing)? If so, make it known. You may be able to serve as a resource, an informal advisor, or a sounding board to your mentor. If not, hone a skill or knowledge in whatever area you're passionate about. It can't hurt you to be an expert just for the sake of serving those who serve you.

Doing what you can to serve or give to your mentor (instead of just taking) shows that you're an active participant in the mentoring process. Know what else you can do? Apply what you're learning to your everyday life, try out advice that resonates with you, and make improvements according to the mentor's feedback. Doing all of this will energize you professionally. Plus, it will show to your mentor (and others) that you're serious about and committed to your own development.

GIVING BACK TO THE FIELD

It's never too early to start identifying opportunities to be a mentor. This is how you can start giving back to your profession. Every lesson learned, conflict encountered, challenge conquered, failure experienced, or mission accomplished contains dos and don'ts that you can pass on to those who are a few steps behind you. Are you an expert yet at this point? No. But you don't need to be an expert to warn someone of any pitfalls and barriers, to point someone to the right direction, to share your experience, and to answer questions so that others can manage their expectations.

Some young careerists give back by teaching, as we both did (and still do). Natalie, while just starting her career at Poudre Valley, served one semester as an instructor of a leadership and management course for the Institute of Business and Medical Careers. Since then, she has taught for various programs, including the University of New Mexico's Anderson Executive MBA program and Brigham Young University's Marriott School MHA program. Likewise, Laurie, at age 25, was invited to teach for a semester an undergraduate course in healthcare administration at Creighton University. She has subsequently held faculty appointments at Clarkson College, Methodist College, and Bellevue University in their respective undergraduate and graduate healthcare administration programs. Currently, she serves as an advisor.

Plus, we both are mentors and frequently volunteer as career coaches, resumé reviewers, and mock interview partners. Our annual early careerist session at ACHE Congress is another way that we extend a hand to those who will be serving the field in the future.

We've all been at that crossroad, not knowing whether we should turn right or left or go straight as we move along our career path. Be that person who reaches out to hand someone a road map. You don't need to tell the person where to go; you just have to show where he or she is at this point in the journey.

Giving back is a good way for you to practice your leadership skills. You are, after all, among the next generation of healthcare leaders. This is your chance to be a role model, a shining example—to others and to yourself. Be the kind of strong mentor that you've always wanted. Be the kind of leader that you'd be proud to follow.

Rookie Mistakes

Putting People on a Pedestal

One way that you could better relate to those in the top ranks (so that you won't be as intimidated to approach them as mentors) is to *not* put them on a pedestal, no matter how much you admire them. They're only human after all.

While attending ACHE Congress many years ago, Laurie sat in the audience of a lecture given by a highly accomplished hospital executive, whom Laurie saw (and still sees) as a role model and thus had put on a pedestal. This executive shared story after story after story about her career—from being overlooked for promotions to being "restructured" by her organization to living through major failures to accepting

→

her own shortcomings. As Laurie listened, she began to see not only the similarity between the executive's experiences and her own but also the authenticity (read: ups and downs) of the executive's journey. She also realized that successful leaders are not magical beings who do everything perfectly all the time and who never grapple with mistakes and difficulties. It was an encouraging lecture for Laurie—as well as an eye-opening one.

Assuming a Mentoring Relationship Without Working for It

Don't be that person who assumes that your colleague's or friend's mentor is also your own—simply because you've met, had a few conversations with, or had been around that mentor. You must earn a mentee position. And it takes a lot more than a meet-and-greet, a five-minute chat or a follow up e-mail, or casual association to establish a mentoring relationship. Be self-aware enough to know when you're overstepping your bounds. And be respectful of the relationships that your friends and colleagues have worked hard to foster—not for your benefit but for their own.

Remember These

- Mentors see the potential in you, and they do what they can to nudge (even push) you toward becoming the person or professional you could be.

- Surround yourself with individuals who don't soothe and coddle your ego all the time. Such a mentor understands that a candid critique will strengthen your character, skills, and performance better than nonstop praise (which may not always be genuine) and agreement can ever do.

- Don't be afraid to ask a CEO or senior executive to be your mentor. They were in your shoes once, so they'll be able to relate to your early career experiences and mentoring needs.

- As a mentee, you can't expect to get helpful advice and guidance from your mentor if you aren't honest about yourself and your concerns, worries, goals, and dreams.

- A board of career advisors is made up of people who serve many purposes and fill many roles, like mentor, advocate or champion, confidante, role model, and even critic.

- Doing what you can to serve or give to your mentor (instead of just taking) shows that you're an active participant in the mentoring process.

PART III

Opening Doors of Opportunity for Yourself

FOR UP AND comers like you, nothing is as constructive as the wisdom of people who have first-hand experiences with the processes and activities you are now undertaking. Just as you wouldn't take resumé-writing tips from someone whose resumé is cluttered with long sentences and unnecessary details, you wouldn't listen to healthcare career advice from someone who has never studied or worked in the field or never held the position you aspire to fill. This theme runs throughout this book, but it's especially apparent in Part III because this is where you take the critical first steps into healthcare management, so you need guidance from those who have worn the shoes you now walk in, so to speak.

Are you a student amid an internship year or the competitive process of searching and applying for internships? A recent graduate going from job interview to job interview? Or a new hire navigating the ins and outs of your first role in the field? Regardless of where you fall in this early-career spectrum, we have you covered. The advice and insights we offer here (in fact, throughout the book) are not only applicable to your situation today but also useful resources for your younger colleagues or even mentees in the future. That's because we include only suggestions and ideas that are classic or timeless, not trendy. When we urge you in 2014 to take full advantage of the exposure to leadership afforded by your internship, for example, we guarantee that in 2024 we will still be promoting that same message (but, of course, tailored for that future environment). The same goes when we insist today that you prepare well for job (and internship) interviews and that you actively pursue (not passively wait for) career opportunities and personal/professional improvement.

These are the same lessons passed on to us by our mentors and the generations of leaders and experts who came before and with us. And now we're sharing them with you in hopes that you will use them not just to get your foot in the door but also to open that door wide for yourself and for others.

CHAPTER 11

Grab That Internship!

*"The distinction between 'assistant' and 'intern' is
a simple one: assistants are paid, interns are not.
But of course interns are paid, in experience."*

Joyce Carol Oates, Novelist

Reading Points

- How It Works

- Applying for an Internship

- Create Your Own Internship

- The End of Internship

ADMINISTRATIVE INTERNSHIPS, FELLOWSHIPS, and residencies. These terms can mean different things in different organizations, but for the sake of simplicity and argument, we're going to consider them all one and the same; we'll refer to them as "internship" in this chapter.

An internship is a bridge between your academic and professional paths, between the end of your schooling and the beginning of your career. For that reason, an internship is both educational and experiential. It requires the intern to perform real-world tasks and to apply classroom techniques—like group discussions, hands-on training, one-on-one coaching, questions and answers, writing a paper, and doing a presentation—to make sense of what has been learned from the internship activities. This is a fantastic setup!

Because an internship exposes you to the highest executive levels, it introduces you to engaging and prominent roles within the organization. It can launch your career, redirect your career path, serve as your fertile learning environment, and assist you in building unprecedented networking relationships. Although often an internship does not materialize into a job, it prepares you for the realities and expectations of the work world—whether your goal as an intern is (1) to prepare yourself to move straight from the classroom to an administrative office or (2) to be groomed as a leader in a specific type of organization.

Here are just some of the things you'd want to gain during an internship:

- Meaningful relationships
- Mentors
- References
- Understanding of operational, clinical, and financial areas of the organization as well as ancillary and support departments or partners
- Working knowledge of important processes, including strategic planning, financial analysis, budgeting, project management, process design and implementation, change initiative, and so on
- Insight into physician arrangements, physician specialties, physician–leadership relationship, and physician referral patterns (what specialties generally consult with other specialties)
- Sense of organizational culture dynamics

- Ability to speak the language of healthcare—that is, general and specific terms, acronyms, shortcuts and slang, and so on
- Understanding of payers (private and public) and payment schemes

Here are just some of the practical things you'd learn:

- How to run meetings for a department, executives, project team, and so on
- How to collaborate with multiple stakeholders
- How to form and lead a team
- How to perform analytics
- How to create a strategic plan
- How to develop, implement, and monitor a process
- How to interview job applicants (and, by extension, how to prepare yourself for a job interview)
- How to spot, correct, and report errors or wrongdoing
- How to embrace or support culture
- How to create and read a pro-forma
- How to write a white paper
- How to procure a piece of equipment or service from RFI to negotiation to signed contract

In this chapter we explain how internships provide invaluable experiences, learning, and connections. We discuss how it works, how to find one, how to take advantage of its many benefits, and how to create internship opportunities where it doesn't exist.

HOW IT WORKS

The structure of an internship can vary from program to program, depending on the culture of the organization, the longevity of the existing program, the vision and direction of the current program preceptor, and so on. Sometimes it takes place during the school semester, something that you could incorporate into your class schedule. Sometimes it takes place the semester after you graduate or during summer break. Sometimes it is paid, and other times it is unpaid.

Typically, it lasts for only one year, but it can accelerate your career by three to five years (perhaps more).

At the beginning of your internship, you may be handed an outline or a schedule for the year. This may include your expected duties, like rounding on different departments for a certain amount of time (like one department for one month, or four departments for three months each). This also may specify the meetings you're expected to attend and the projects you're expected to complete. At the completion of your internship, you may be required to write a paper and/or do a formal presentation in front of the program preceptor, organizational leadership, department directors, or other personnel.

The essence of internship is exposure. Count on being introduced to the inner workings of departments and the organization as a whole, the community at large, the movers and shakers inside and outside the organization, myriad change initiatives, bureaucracy and politicking, all levels of personnel, and so much more. Take advantage of all of it.

The harsh reality is that, in one year, your "seat at the table" will end, and you will no longer have an all-access pass to senior management (until, of course, that day when you become part of that team). So while you're serving as intern, gain as much real-world knowledge and experience, maximize your exposure and proximity to experienced leaders, try new things and develop new skills, and look for or create opportunities that can extend your tenure or turn your internship into a full-time position. For example, when Natalie was a fellow at a health system, she was charged with designing the organization's retail strategic plan.

When she presented the plan to the board at the end of her fellowship, she impressed them enough that she was hired as the full-time director of retail services.

Tips for Taking Advantage of Your Internship

- *Get to know the role of your preceptor.* Similar to a manager, a preceptor is the person you will report to throughout your intern year. The preceptor answers your questions, helps you gain access where and when you need it, gives you feedback, and guides your every step. You will likely meet with your preceptor regularly—often weekly—so that he or she can check on your progress, keep you on track, brainstorm project ideas, and give advice and direction. Sometimes, a private debriefing with your preceptor is necessary. For example, after you've observed certain occurrences (like critical decision-making moments, community interactions, strategy or policy changes, or disagreements), you may ask questions about what happened, why it happened, and whether there's a historical context or precedent to what occurred. This is one of the ways you can learn about the inner workings of the organization.

  Understand that your preceptor is expecting you to have many questions, so don't be shy or afraid to ask away! The preceptor (along with everyone else in the organization) assumes you are sharp, prepared, and thoughtful but not necessarily someone who knows everything. In fact, she or he might think you know less than you actually do given that interns have different backgrounds and have varying degrees of experiences and thus know-how. Despite what you know or don't know, the preceptor is expecting that you'll meet your deadlines, produce good work, and ask for clarifications when you are unsure.

If you gel well with your preceptor, he or she can become a valuable reference during your internship and even a longstanding mentor after your internship. Natalie and her preceptor, for example, have remained good friends for years, and he has proven to be an invaluable mentor, colleague, and friend. She relies on him to offer his perspective and general guidance when she faces tough situations. Because he is genuinely proud of her and views her success as an extension of his own, she shares news of her accomplishments with him and acknowledges and thanks him for his countless and selfless contributions to her growth.

- *Sit down and interview a leader from a different department every month.* One is great, but more is better. Take them to lunch or coffee, and pick their brain. Ask them how they got to where they are, what they do, and how their specific part (like overall responsibilities, departmental goals, daily duties) fits into the general whole of the organization. Such a conversation will give you insight into how the organization operates, part by part and inside out. Plus, it will help you define what service or operational area you'd like to learn more about or specialize in once your program ends.

  Don't forget to ask the leader if you could add him or her to your network. Most important, volunteer to help with projects or tasks in the executive's department if your schedule allows or if your preceptor approves. Volunteering will not only help you initiate a relationship with the leader but also give you the opportunity to learn about her or his area.

  If you sit down with one executive per month, by the end of the year you will have 12 new experts in your network with whom you could build a relationship. Sustain these networking relationships.

And don't forget the doctors and other clinicians! Approach them, too. Get acquainted with their perspective. How do they view administration? What can leaders do to better serve patients and their families, to involve the clinical side in organizational initiatives, to improve relationships between physicians and the hospital?

- *Keep an internship journal.* Jot down your daily activities, key learning moments, progress made on your projects, tidbits of information, and pearls of wisdom. You might find that you'll reference this record for years to come!

- *Dive into as many organizational areas as possible.* If your internship plan doesn't include a department or unit, specialty, service line, program, or initiative you'd like to get involved in and learn about, ask your preceptor if it could be added. It's likely that the organization will allow you to go for whatever piques your interest. In fact, some internship programs give interns carte blanche or full access to almost every part of the organization, enabling interns to observe and even participate in the activities or projects of the units. If this is the case, ask to be assigned to every conceivable area possible. You could be a member of the performance improvement team, sit in on governing board meetings, shadow an ER manager during a full shift, or assist the COO and her staff with the implementation of a new policy.

By diving in, you can whittle down your list of the areas you want to work in and don't want to work in once you become a practicing healthcare manager. For example, if you spent an internship month working on quality improvement projects and tasks and absolutely hated that kind of detailed work, now you know not to pursue a position that heavily relies on that skill set.

Again, self-awareness is critical at this point. If you understand your own strengths and weaknesses, you can better steer the direction of your career path.

There is no better time than during an internship to immerse yourself in myriad experiences, determine what you like and don't like about an area in particular and the world of healthcare in general, learn a lot and from the best, and ask for guidance and feedback. This is also the time to hone your interpersonal, listening, and critical thinking skills and to practice your ability to follow directions, execute plans, and try new things or take risks.

APPLYING FOR AN INTERNSHIP

The rigors and prestige of many internship programs make acceptance into these programs highly selective. Plus, there are always more student candidates than internship positions, so open spots are tough to find. If you are facing this dilemma, apply to multiple internship programs; if you're willing, apply to those that are out of your immediate area.

1. *Application form.* This is usually lengthy, so be patient and fill it out completely and accurately. Natalie has been on selection panels and has witnessed entire applications thrown out because of minor spelling errors or incomplete sections. Because there are so many applications, most selection committees are not shy about pitching those that are less than perfect. Take your time when filling out this application, have someone else proofread your work, and send out only your best effort.

2. *Essay.* It's totally appropriate for you to ask someone who is further along in his or her career (like a mentor

or older colleague) to look over your essay—not just for grammar or syntax but also for overall content. How well does your essay reflect real-world expectations and healthcare realities? Does it make sense in the current healthcare environment? If you are still a student, your experience in the real-world trenches is limited, so allow your experienced colleague to guide you. Your essay will invariably be stronger after you make the edits suggested by your colleague.

Tap into your network or board of career advisors and invite some of them to speak with you candidly about your strengths and weaknesses as well as your chances of landing available internship opportunities. Use their feedback to answer essay questions like "What do you hope to get out of this internship?"

Often, applications include one general essay question or a series of three or four questions. Give each one the attention it deserves. You may use key terms—such as commitment, self-discipline, tenacity or perseverance, character, experience, learning orientation, service, and meaningful or valuable work—to bolster your arguments. If needed, dig into your old high school guidebooks about how to structure sentences, paragraphs, and essays. Selection panels assess application essays on their grammar and syntax just as much as on their content. Keep in mind that a well-thought-out essay can be used, with only slight modifications (tailored to fit the organization's internship requirements), from application to application.

3. *References.* Choose your references wisely! Ask people who (a) have seen your work and know your potential to perform at high levels if given a great opportunity and (b) will speak well about your skills and knowledge as well

as your character. Some internship programs require that you submit a letter of reference, while others ask that you provide the contact information for your references so that the programs can call your references directly. Either way, get permission from your references and give them a heads up that they could be contacted. No one wants to be surprised or caught unprepared to vouch for you. Lastly, before you furnish a list of references, make sure that the people on the list are still alive, still willing to give you a reference, and still can be reached at their listed phone number. A fantastic reference with out-of-date contact information isn't worth a thing and is embarrassing!

4. *Interview.* There are so many candidates for internships that a phone interview will almost always be done first to weed out the competition. A face-to-face interview will follow. (See Chapter 12 for more discussion on interviewing; some of our suggested strategies in that chapter—especially how you present yourself and interact with the interviewers—apply to internship interviews as well.)

Final thoughts on applying for internships: Apply early and apply often. Internships are cyclical and usually run from July to July; they may be awarded as far in advance as the beginning of the calendar year. It's prudent to start looking for internships for the following year just after summer of the preceding year. Application due dates vary from program to program. If you are applying to many (which you should be doing), create a spreadsheet to track the process and due dates for each program.

Lean on Your School Network to Find Internship Opportunities

Talk to the director of your health administration program to find out if he or she knows of alumni whom you could approach for an internship opportunity; it's a bonus if they work for an organization in which you want to intern. Ask second-year students where they interned their first year. Ask recent graduates where they interned while in school. Contact your network, board of career advisors (if any), professors, and classmates for suggestions. Once word spreads that you are seeking guidance, opportunities or leads may come your way. (As we've mentioned in earlier chapters, we don't advise you to get in touch with your networking contacts only for the purpose of asking them for a favor. Reach out to them only after you've already built rapport; otherwise, they'll feel used and will disengage from your network.)

You may check out these resources as well:

- Alumni association of your college or university
- State chapters of associations, like the American College of Healthcare Executives, Medical Group Management Association, and Healthcare Financial Management Association
- Local or national health systems online job boards
- Career section of the website of trade organizations and healthcare associations
- State hospital associations' careerist resources
- Human resources departments

CREATE YOUR OWN INTERNSHIP

If you can't move across the country or to a different town for a few months of internship, or if you can't spend an entire semester getting paid nothing or next to nothing, you can still make an internship work for you and your unique situation. How? Walk into the human resources department of the hospital or healthcare organization you would like to be a part of, and ask. It's not common and it's bold, but this step can pay off.

When Laurie was completing her MHA, her program hosted a visiting lecturer one evening—the CEO of a local health system. Several months later, as she approached the final semester of her program, she cold-called the CEO to inquire about internship opportunities. He offered her a semester-long, part-time internship. If the story stopped here, it would be good enough, but it got better. Halfway through that internship, the VP of clinic operations was terminated. Laurie, who was aware she was very light on qualifications for this big role, asked the CEO if she could apply for the position anyway. He took a chance and gave her the nod. She became the next VP of clinic operations for the organization—thanks to the internship that brought her there.

If you don't have the time to participate in an in-person internship, you could still pursue a learning opportunity by, first, contacting the director of human resources for the organization you want to serve. Ask to interview the director for one hour about the areas you're interested in. Select an area based on the information you obtained, and then develop a working relationship with the head of that area. Volunteer your free services for a certain amount of time (like one hour once a week for three months). What organization would turn down this offer: "I would love an internship, but I have a full-time job. But I'd like a chance to work with you on a project. I'm available a few hours a week for the next few months. I can work for free"?

If this approach doesn't work, you could at least forge networking relationships and add the organization as a reference.

Job Shadowing

A casual, but no less valuable, way to garner real-world experience is job shadowing. Obtained through the same methods as landing an internship, job shadowing entails following a professional around at work for a few hours or a few days. This is a great way to get your foot in the door to future internship and full-time positions as well as to meet people you could add to your network. If you shadow someone once per semester throughout your two-year graduate program, by the time you finish school you'll have gained four new experiences and four new networking contacts. That's a huge payoff for a small investment of time!

THE END OF INTERNSHIP

All good things come to an end. Because most internships do not lead to permanent positions, you must develop a plan for the next adventure in your career. About four to six months before you complete your internship, begin your job hunt. For example, Natalie approached her internship very strategically. About six months into it, she started looking and applying for jobs. This way, she thought, her transition from internship to employment would be seamless and that she would be gainfully employed by a health-care organization by the time her fellowship was over. Luckily, her internship led to a position in the same organization (see her earlier story of how she became the director of retail services).

If you like the organization where you interned, speak to your preceptor or someone else about any potential fits for your skill set. If no positions are available or will open up in the near future, look elsewhere. You know that network that you've worked so hard to build up and maintain? Now is the time to use it. Ask for appropriate references, update your resumé (add all the awesome things you did during your internship), scan the job ads, and fill out applications. Good luck!

Remember These

- An internship prepares you for the realities and expectations of the work world—whether your goal as an intern is (1) to prepare yourself to move straight from the classroom to an administrative office or (2) to be groomed as a leader in a specific type of organization.

- While you're serving as intern, gain as much real-world knowledge and experience, maximize your exposure and proximity to experienced leaders, try new things and develop new skills, and look for or create opportunities that can extend your tenure or turn your internship into a full-time position.

- Understand that your preceptor is expecting you to have many questions, so don't be shy or afraid to ask away! The preceptor (along with everyone else in the organization) assumes you are sharp, prepared, and thoughtful but not necessarily someone who knows everything.

- By diving into as many organizational areas as possible, you can whittle down your list of the areas you want to work in and don't want to work in once you become a practicing healthcare manager.

- The rigors and prestige of many internship programs make acceptance into these programs highly selective. Plus, there are always more student candidates than internship positions, so open spots are tough to find.

- Take your time when filling out an internship application, have someone else proofread your work, and send out only your best effort. A slight mistake or an incomplete form could hurt your chances.

- Because most internships do not lead to permanent positions, you must develop a plan for the next adventure in your career. About four to six months before you complete your internship, begin your job hunt.

CHAPTER 12

Master the Job Interview

"Be so good they can't ignore you."

—*Steve Martin, Actor*

Reading Points

- The Preparation Stage
- The Interview Stage
- The Follow-Up Stage
- Salary and Benefits Negotiation

THE MOST COMMONLY asked questions we receive from new health administration graduates who attend our ACHE Congress seminar revolve around the job interview. It makes sense. After all, you can't start a career path until you land a job. And you can't land a job if you don't ace that interview. Plus, often you can't move on to another organization or apply for a bigger and better position without going through the interview process. To a careerist, the interview is as inevitable and as life changing as failure.

By the time you sit for the interview—the face-to-face, question-and-answer, resumé explanation portion of the process—you should already have done a lot of leg work to present yourself in the best light. That's because the interview is merely one stage, sandwiched between the preparation and the follow-up stages. Successful interviewers know that this much work goes into the process. As such, they master all components of each stage, leaving nothing to chance.

Preparation. Interview. Follow up. Let's dig into each of them in this chapter.

THE PREPARATION STAGE

Just as you shouldn't show up to a certification exam without having studied, you shouldn't show up to a job interview without having prepared. This is a must to ensure that, during the interview, you can respond thoughtfully to questions, feel and look professional but at ease, articulate relevant job experiences and qualifications, pose informed questions, and ultimately convince the interview panel that you are the right person for the position.

At the prep stage, gather as much information as you can— not just on the job qualifications and responsibilities but also on the organization and the interviewers. Take copious notes. Review those notes over and over. Memorize details if you can.

Research the Organization

During an interview, nothing is worse for you than being clueless about the organization you're interviewing with. From the organization's perspective, you don't care enough about becoming a member of their team because you didn't even bother to get to know them. From the interviewer's perspective, you are wasting everybody's time.

Don't leave that impression. That's as bad as a no call, no show, which burns bridges.

So what should you know specifically? Learn the organization's mission, vision, and values. Relate them to your own beliefs as you study. In the past ten years, neither of us remembers a time when the interviewer didn't ask, "Which one of our values resonated with you the most?" Know how to answer that and similar questions.

Familiarize yourself with the history, type of services, awards, patient mix, and locations of the organization. Has the hospital been a part of the community since 1940, or did it just open five years ago after separating from a regional system? Is it an acute care, a specialty care, or an outpatient facility, a for-profit or not-for-profit? Does it have an ER, a NICU, an urgent care clinic? What awards or recognitions has it earned lately? What system is it affiliated with? Is it freestanding? When you know these details, you can better weigh job-related decisions, such as transfer opportunities—that is, if you're open to moving to other locations within the larger organization.

Start your research with the company's website, and then branch out from there to industry publications and even Google searches (using the organization's name as well as its top leadership). Check its social media pages, which document its current news and events as well as showcase its overall culture and personality. Ask your networking contacts if they know any current or past employees of the organization. Tap your former undergraduate or graduate school classmates to see whether anyone has interned or worked there.

Take the time to do your research, and do it well. (Natalie, for example, gives herself five to seven days to properly prepare for an interview.) The knowledge (or lack of knowledge) you bring to the interview itself speaks volumes about you and your intention to secure a second interview and ultimately a job. We argue that this preparation is just as important (if not more so) as your performance during the actual interview.

Research the Interview Panel

Whether your interview panel consists of one or ten people, you should educate yourself about the members of this panel. Doing so shows that you are interested in and care about these individuals (not to mention the job itself), are personable, and are professional. Furthermore, it allies you to the interviewers and generally makes you approachable and memorable. Two good sources of this information are the organization's online staff directory (if you can access it) and LinkedIn (many professionals have profiles). Google also works.

Learn each panelist's name, title or role, responsibilities, and background. Background information serves as conversation fodder, which helps you create an instant connection with panelists. For example, you may find that one or some of them went to the same school, came from the same state, or volunteer for the same charitable cause as you. That's common ground you can use to strike up a conversation or break the ice. When interviewers are able to relate to you, they can picture themselves working with you.

Remembering people's names is invaluable in any situation, but more so during an interview. Address interviewers by name when you respond, such as "Well, Mary, I'm glad you asked that question!" or "Thanks, Bob, I agree with that philosophy." This makes the interview more intimate as opposed to impersonal. Natalie once interviewed with a ten-person panel. Because she did her research on each person and matched each face with his or her name, she knew everyone even before they introduced themselves. She tacked on the interviewer's name to her answers, something that wowed the panel because, in their view, she had just learned their name. It was a savvy move that convinced them she has a quick mind that absorbs a lot of information even in a stressful situation. That gave her an edge over the other applicants. And guess what? She got the job.

Practice Your Elevator Speech

An elevator speech is a brief (about 30 to 60 seconds or long enough to deliver during an elevator ride) description of who you are, what you do, what you're passionate about, what you want to accomplish, and other details specific to your career path. It's a high-level summary of your personal brand. It should include your career goals and aspirations. That's a lot of important stuff to fit into half a minute! But sometimes those seconds feel like forever when you don't know what else to say.

Your elevator speech shouldn't be a regurgitation of your resumé. Boring. The interviewers have the resumé in front of them, so no need to repeat the information. Share something about your passion and experiences, something that's not included or hard to explain on a resumé. But limit the personal details you include. No pet names, favorite color, and silly or irrelevant information. Here's a sample elevator speech: "I'm a Tennessee native who is passionate about leadership development, clinical quality improvement, and collaborating with healthcare practitioners to maximize efficiency in patient care processes. My studies and internship experiences show that I thrive in small organizations and communities, where I can readily observe the impact of my efforts and build meaningful relationships with fellow employees and local stakeholders." None of this appears on a resumé, and no non-work-related details are included.

The first question just about every interviewer poses is, "Tell me a little about yourself." If you come prepared to deliver a well-written and well-practiced elevator speech, you can relax when you hear this question. That calm and in-control demeanor then sets the tone for the rest of your interview. You're already batting a thousand! You've got the first question right! Nice start; it builds confidence.

Conduct a Mock interview

"Practice makes perfect" applies to shooting free throws and playing the piano just as well as it does to interviewing. Start holding mock interviews at least five days in advance of your interview. Here's a guideline for doing this right:

1. *Recruit a reliable, serious partner to play the interviewer role.* This person may be a family member, friend, mentor, or a member of your board of career advisors. Make sure he or she takes this exercise seriously and won't break character at any time during the interview. To add to the authenticity, ask the person to wear business attire.

2. *Set some rules.* No joking around. No time-outs. No do-overs or mulligans. No getting up to answer the phone or the door or a text or an e-mail; in fact, set aside a whole hour without distractions. And that goes for your mock interviewer as well. Tell everyone you have an appointment so that they don't come visit or call/text. The only effective way to practice is to treat the process as real.

3. *Use real-world interview questions.* Have your mock interviewer ask questions taken from your own interview experiences, from a friend or colleague who recently had a big interview, from human resources (HR) departments, and so on. These questions probe your job qualifications; skills, knowledge, and abilities; specific past and current experiences; character traits; leadership style or approaches; attitude about various things; strengths and weaknesses; and so on.

   Here's how you can collect real-world questions, a strategy that has worked for Natalie: The moment you walk out of an interview, immediately jot down as many of the questions you were asked while they are still fresh in your head. In addition, you can call the

HR department of any random organization to inquire if you can obtain a list of general interview questions. You may also ask friends who recently had interviews for the questions they were asked. Create a personal list or database to organize your collection for future reference. You'll find that the questions are pretty similar from one organization to the next.

Think of unexpected questions as well, and formulate answers for those. This way, you can show the real interviewer how well you've prepared; it may also help you get unstuck if you encounter a difficult question during the actual interview.

4. *Practice your recovery.* Flubbing on a question is highly likely during an interview. It is a stressful situation, and you're expected to be "on" the whole time. A mock interview is the best time to practice saving yourself from misspeaking, giving wrong or conflicting information, not answering satisfactorily, getting stuck on a question, or any other errors. Learn how to listen to yourself and quickly pick up on your own flubs so that you can get back on track. Learn how to pause methodically so that you can collect your thoughts before you speak.

5. *Dress the part.* You don't have to don a skirt/pantsuit or a suit and tie, but we urge you to do so. It puts you in the interviewing frame of mind. At this time, you could break in the new outfit and/or shoes you bought.

6. *Practice modulating the speed, volume, cadence, and tone of your voice.* You might have a fabulous answer to every interview question, but if you talk too fast, too loud, or too soft; lower or raise your voice for no reason; mumble and garble your words, your interviewer won't understand what you're saying (let alone hear your brilliance). Practice speaking slowly, enunciate, and use an upbeat tone. This shows your confidence, interest, and sense of comfort.

We've never met a person who didn't speak too fast when nervous or too soft when lacking confidence.

7. *Ask your mock interviewer for feedback afterward.* This is self-explanatory. The important thing to remember is to act on the feedback immediately. For example, if the feedback is, "you beat around the bush too much" or "you talk so loud," you should be more direct with your responses and you should adjust your volume at your next mock interview.

THE INTERVIEW STAGE

The day has arrived: interview day. Don't be nervous! Okay, maybe being a little nervous is a good thing; it means you care. Because you care, you must pay attention to every detail. Assuming you've prepared properly, nothing but the details are standing between you and a great interview. (Note that the discussion below is geared toward face-to-face interviews, as that's the most common form, but we touch on phone interviews at the end of this section.)

- *Dress professionally but comfortably.* This seems contradictory, but hear us out. If you bought new shoes and clothes, cut their tags and break them in a few days before the big day. Don't wait until the day to find out that the shoes are too narrow or the shirt is too scratchy. An uncomfortable outfit will only distract you from bringing your A game and hurt your chance to shine.
- *Bring a notebook or padfolio, pens, extra copies of your resumé, and business cards if you have them.* The notebook or padfolio and business cards must be free of dirt, doodles and scribbles, stickers, and anything else that makes them look unclean. Copies of your resumé must be unwrinkled and crisp. Take notes during the interview, because it

shows you're paying attention and keeping up with the flow of information.

- *Carry your things in an organized manner.* That might sound like an insignificant, micromanaging advice, but we assure you it matters. Picture yourself walking into the interview room while fumbling with your belongings. Your purse, brief case, or manbag slung haphazardly on your shoulder; your notebook or pad and pens and resumés and business cards bulge out of your one hand; your cell phone (which you should tuck in your bag or leave in your car) and coffee cup and keys or coat threaten to jump out of the other hand. Then you have to walk across the room while juggling all these things, hoping nothing falls out. Then you have to dump all these things. Then you have to straighten yourself out. All that before you even shake hands with the interviewer. That's not a very graceful first impression, is it?

- *Smile!* Smile from entrance to exit. Smile at the receptionists, the security guards, the people you encounter in the elevators and hallways, the person who calls you into the interview room, the interviewers, the other candidates, and everyone else in between. It brightens your face, and it puts everyone in a good mood. Most important, it shows you're glad to be there, ready to engage, and thankful for the opportunity.

- *Beware of your body language.* Shake hands firmly and look people directly in the eye, because that shows professionalism and willingness to engage. Watch your mannerisms (e.g., flailing arms, blinking too much) as you speak, because they could distract your audience. Other distractions include yawning, stretching, slouching, laughing or talking too loud, looking around the room instead of at the speaker, and having a blank expression on your face.

- *Use your mock interview experience as a jumping-off point for your responses.* If you properly practiced and did it enough times, no questions (even the unexpected or on the fly) should faze you. Sometimes your practice questions match the actual questions. But often they are different. You should be able to pull answers from your mock interviews and use those as a base or frame of reference for actual questions such as "Is there anything about you that we haven't talked about that you'd like me to know?"

  If you get stuck on a question, take a quick moment to gain your composure. Restate the question aloud and speak slowly, pausing or using fillers if you need to buy time. "That's a great question, Mark, give me a second to think about that. [Pause] I would say that. . . [Pause]." This might give you five or ten extra seconds, but it looks like your gears are in motion, thinking of the appropriate response. That's ok; no one should penalize you for thinking things through. But don't take too long, as your interview doesn't last forever. Often, the answers come once you start speaking; again, rely on your extensive preparation. Take a deep breath; you've got this.

- *Ask follow-up and wrap-up questions.* Interviewers almost always give you a chance to ask questions. Interviews are as much an opportunity for the organization to get to know you as for you to get to know the employer, its people, and the open position. Always prepare two to three well-thought-out questions to ask when it's your turn (at the end). You could ask job-specific questions that were not covered earlier or you wanted to clarify. You could ask general questions about the organization that you found interesting while doing your research. You could inquire about the culture, the leadership's vision for the future, the organization's community involvement, and so on.

Keep a pad and pen with you at all times; you never know, a question about the organization may pop in your head while you're grocery shopping or eating dinner with friends.

Embrace the chance to turn the tables for a few minutes. It will show you have the initiative to do some research, you're interested and curious, and you're engaged. Natalie, who has interviewed many dozens of applicants, almost never hires anybody who didn't pose any wrap-up questions. Why? Because not having questions is the quickest way to communicate that you don't care what this organization does and believes in, that you're there to earn a paycheck and do nothing else. (See Exhibit 12.1 for examples of questions to ask.)

- *Seek common ground.* As we mentioned earlier, you and the interviewer could find a commonality that builds instant rapport that, in turn, changes the one-sided interview into a friendly, less intimidating conversation ("I see that you sit on the Big Brothers Big Sisters board here in Atlanta, Susan. I had a little sister during my four years of undergrad! It was such an amazing learning experience for me."). Find that common ground and sustain that connection. Not only would it make the interview fun (or at least not dry) and memorable for both of you, but it would make the interviewer envision you as part of his or her team. You know you are nailing the interview when the interviewer is talking as much as you are!
- *Showcase your personal brand.* More than ever, organizations are hiring for fit—not just in terms of skill and aptitude but also in terms of interests and attitudes. If you are able to share and showcase your brand during the interview (through your elevator speech, demeanor, and interaction), you are boosting your chances of being a top contender for the job.

Exhibit 12.1 Sample Wrap-Up Questions

- What would my first 30 to 60 days look like in this role?

- What attributes are most valuable to succeeding in this role?

- What type of manager do you consider yourself?

- What are the current strategic goals of the organization? What about for your team/department?

- What three words would you use to describe the organization's culture?

Phone Interviews

When you think of the interview process, think of its three ascending levels. First is the resumé. That's when you send in your resumé and cover letter, which are then scanned, passed on to, and decided on by various people, one of whom makes a call back to you. The resumé level is critical because if you don't look good on paper, you won't advance to the next level. Simple as that. Make sure your resumé makes an impact on screeners by being descriptive but streamlined, easy to read and follow (use bullet points and reverse chronological order), and reflective of your personal brand (Giang 2013).

Second is the phone interview, which is the gatekeeper level that screens you and other candidates and decides whether you can proceed to the next stage. Third is the face-to-face interview, which is the ultimate level.

As you can see, the phone interview is an important step toward a job offer. It's rare for an organization to skip this level—that is, spend time and resources interviewing someone face to face simply from an initial scan of a resumé. So prepare as much for a phone interview as you would for a face to face.

During a phone interview, dress to impress and smile even if the interviewer can't see you. Like we said, act *as if* and let them hear you smile. When you do, you will feel great. And that will transmit through the wires. Address the interviewer by name, and strive to find a common ground to establish a quick connection. You don't have to watch your body language, but you do have to modulate your voice and speak clearly. Take notes, as these will help you come up with follow-up questions.

Hold the interview in a quiet space. Use a landline, if you can, as cell reception is often unreliable or spotty; you don't want to get cut off in the middle of the interview or to hear static. Block off the interview time and notify others who share the same space (including your roommate, significant other, toddler's babysitter, parents, or coworkers) to prevent sudden noises. Treat the phone interview with the utmost respect and professionalism, as you would a face-to-face interview.

One of the benefits of a phone interview is that if you need to compose yourself or think of an answer, you could ask for a question repeat. "I'm sorry, Arthur, I didn't hear the question. Would you mind repeating it?" This could grant you the extra seconds you need to gather your thoughts.

THE FOLLOW-UP STAGE

Sales people often say that the fortune is in the follow-up. In the world of healthcare leadership, the fortune and the prestige of landing that new role relies heavily on the follow-up.

Timing is everything here. A handwritten note three weeks after the interview is just about pointless. But a handwritten note that arrives within 24 hours or an e-mail sent within one hour after the interview can be gold. If a same-day note is at all humanly possible, do it. That or a next-day note will make a positive impression on those you spoke to.

Follow-up every interview, every time. Always have a note card and envelope ready, already addressed and stamped. Write the note and drop it in the mailbox on your way home. See Exhibit 12.2 for a sample follow-up note.

Exhibit 12.2 Sample Thank You Note

Dear Ms. Winston,

Thank you for the opportunity to interview for the role of Operations Coordinator for Radiation Oncology. It was a pleasure meeting you and your team and learning more about your organization. After touring the department and meeting a few of your staff, I feel confident that I can contribute to your goals for growth in the coming year. I am looking forward to hearing from you soon, and I would be honored to be a part of the ABC Health System team.

Cordially,

Natalie

Likewise, send a follow-up note even if you didn't get the job. Differentiate yourself from the crowd, and send a handwritten note or an e-mail to each panelist upon hearing that you are now out of the running. Convey your gratitude for the opportunity to be considered, and wish each one well in their future endeavors. Such a gracious follow-up makes an impact and communicates the strength of your character. This will remind them of who you are and leave the door open for conversations or roles that might come up down the road.

Networking and interviewing overlap in so many ways, and this is one of those ways. Even if the interview does not end in a job offer, it may lead to you gaining new network contacts—especially after the note you sent to each panelist. For example, Natalie interviewed at the Mayo Clinic but didn't end up getting the job, although she thought the interview went really well. It turned out she was right; she ended up being second to a woman with a PhD who was on sabbatical from the Mayo Clinic. As soon as she heard the news, she mailed a follow-up note to the panelists, thanking each of them for their kindness and the opportunity to interview as well as acknowledging how much she enjoyed the process. She was able to turn that experience into a networking relationship with the same people who interviewed her. What's more, she gained additional great interview experience.

Remember, this is a small industry. Your goodwill and kindness spread, but so does your apathy or lack of caring.

SALARY AND BENEFITS NEGOTIATION

A 2013 survey found that 49 percent of the full-time employees who responded to the survey never negotiated their initial job offer. Of those who did negotiate, older professional workers (aged 35 or over) tended to do it more than their younger counterparts (aged 18 to 34) did (CareerBuilder 2013). Time to change this pattern, folks!

First, do you know that negotiation is an option? Almost always, except in cases where the salary and benefits are fixed (like jobs in the public sector, including the military). Second, do you think it's a waste of time? Never. Don't be bashful when it comes to your livelihood or your worth. You're not being overly aggressive if you demand fair pay and benefits for your hard work, experience, and qualifications. In fact, the same survey said that 45 percent of the companies that participated were open to first-offer negotiations. Educate yourself. Research the market and your industry to find out average compensation or level/job-specific wages. Be aware that organizations almost always extend an initial offer that is less than the highest amount they are willing to pay. So go ahead, talk money! Take Laurie's example when she made her own case—twice.

In her first leadership role after graduate school, Laurie negotiated $10,000 more than her initial offer. Her justifications for the higher salary included her master's degree, which wasn't a requirement of the position; her recent experience in a four-month internship within the clinic, where she completed a full assessment of the clinic's network; and her knowledge of clinic operations, which eliminated the need to train her.

In her current role, Laurie negotiated a higher base compensation as well as an allocation of personal days to invest in maintaining an active presence on the speaking circuit. This not only affords her the opportunity to flex her entrepreneurial muscle (through continuing to accept select speaking and leadership development engagements) but also boosts the credibility and visibility of her employer.

So when's the time to negotiate? *Not* during the first interview. In fact, don't even bring up compensation at that point because you would come across as someone who's just in it for the money! Do it *after* the organization makes you an offer. Accept the job, and then go home and do some research (if you haven't already) on market wages and benefits for your job title, level or grade, skills and other qualifications, and job responsibilities—within and outside your industry, profession, and even state. Members of your network may have already given you clues on what ballpark figure to expect, but you want to be armed with solid, market-based information (not hearsay) when you negotiate. Whatever salary and benefits (or perks) you decide to counter the initial offer with, make sure they are not so unreasonable or way beyond expectations that the negotiation becomes hostile or uncompromising. You want to keep the dialogue civil and open.

Make a list of your justifications for the increase. What extra qualifications and training do you have? What unique value are you adding to the position and the department? Tie your request to only objective reasons (like "I have extensive experience, an advanced degree, and certifications") and never to subjective criteria (like "I want my spouse to be able to stay home" or "I need a new car"). If your new employer's response to a raise is "no," ask if any other nonsalary concessions can be extended to you. These may include a professional development stipend, relocation expense reimbursement, additional personal or vacation days, or partial flex or telecommute arrangements.

Bottom line: Be prepared to negotiate by doing your research and writing down your justifications—and make your counter offer within the timeframe given (usually a few days). Know your worth, even if you're just starting out.

Remember These

- The interview is merely one stage, sandwiched between the preparation and the follow-up stages.
- Preparation is a must to ensure that, during the interview, you can respond thoughtfully to questions, feel and look professional but at ease, articulate relevant job experiences and qualifications, pose informed questions, and ultimately convince the interview panel that you are the right person for the position.
- Take the time to do your research, and do it well. The knowledge (or lack of knowledge) you bring to the interview itself speaks volumes about you and your intention to secure a second interview and ultimately a job.
- Address interviewers by name when you respond. This makes the interview more intimate as opposed to impersonal.
- An elevator speech is a brief description of who you are, what you do, what you're passionate about, what you want to accomplish, and other details specific to your career path.
- Hold mock interviews at least five days in advance of your interview.
- Think of the interview process in terms of its three ascending levels: (1) resumé level, (2) phone interview level, and (3) face-to-face interview level.
- Timing is everything in follow-up. A handwritten note three weeks after the interview is just about pointless. But a handwritten note that arrives within 24 hours or an e-mail sent within one hour after the interview can be gold.
- Networking and interviewing overlap in so many ways, and this is one of those ways. Even if the interview does

not end in a job offer, it may lead to you gaining new
network contacts.

- Don't be bashful when it comes to your livelihood
  or your worth. You're not being overly aggressive if
  you demand fair pay and benefits for your hard work,
  experience, and qualifications.

- Don't negotiate your salary and benefits during the first
  interview. Do it *after* the organization makes you an
  offer.

REFERENCES

CareerBuilder. 2013. "Forty-Nine Percent of Workers Do Not Negotiate Job Offers."
Posted August 21. www.careerbuilder.com/share/aboutus/pressreleasesdetail
.aspx?sd=8/21/2013&id=pr777&ed=12/31/2013.

Giang, V. 2013. "19 Reasons Why This Is an Excellent Resume." Posted November
7. www.businessinsider.com/why-this-is-an-excellent-resume-2013-11.

ADDITIONAL RESOURCES

Shin, L. 2013. "New Grads, Here's How To Negotiate Your Salary." *Forbes*. www.
forbes.com/sites/laurashin/2013/06/26/new-grads-heres-how-to-negotiate
-your-salary/.

Smith, J. 2013. "How to Ace the 50 Most Common Interview Questions." *Forbes*.
www.forbes.com/sites/jacquelynsmith/2013/01/11/how-to-ace-the-50
-most-common-interview-questions/.

CHAPTER 13

Own and Manage Your Career Path

"I want to look back on my career and be proud of the work,
be proud that I tried everything."

—*Jon Stewart, Host,* The Daily Show

Reading Points

- Don't Underestimate the Value of an Entry-Level Job
- Do Make It Happen
- Don't Get Comfortable
- Do Chart a Career Path
- Do Act *As If*
- Do Stand Out
- Do Make the Boss Look Good
- Do Win Employees Over, Especially Those Older Than You

EVERY STEP YOU take toward being an accomplished health-care leader is important. Every step is a learning experience, an opportunity to network and build lasting connections, and an occasion to prepare yourself for the next level and beyond. Take advantage of each step.

Remember what we said way back in Chapter 1? Let's remind you: One of the benefits of being self-aware is gaining an intimate knowledge of your character, strengths and weaknesses, and interpersonal style. When you have this understanding, you can better act. That is, instead of shoehorning yourself into a role simply because it pays well, is prestigious, or is what everyone expects for you, you can chart a career path that suits you best. Doing work that is both meaningful and rewarding is the holy grail for career-minded individuals. That's way more important than any title or pay grade. (Sadly, we know too many well-titled and highly compensated people who are miserable at their jobs.) So get to know yourself; chart a career path; take the initiative to land opportunities, challenge yourself, and stand out; and present your best self and do your best work to stay on your path.

In this chapter, we present the dos and don'ts of managing your career—specifically, at the early stages. Here, we revisit concepts and strategies that we've discussed in earlier chapters. We also provide examples and recommendations taken from real-world experiences.

DON'T UNDERESTIMATE THE VALUE OF AN ENTRY-LEVEL JOB

After completing her undergraduate degree, Laurie took a job as an administrative assistant for the clinic network of a large health system. A glamorous role? Definitely not. A high-paying position? Hardly. At the time, she was pursuing her MHA degree full time and was chomping at the bit to move on. She wanted more. She felt like she was not undertaking worthwhile work, and she couldn't wait to realize her potential. (See also Chapter 8 for another facet to this story.)

In hindsight, Laurie recognizes that the two years she spent in that role taught her things she couldn't have gleaned from a textbook, a case study, or a classroom lecture. She saw how physician practices *really* operated, how every role in the practice functioned, what the physicians did day to day, what their needs and priorities were, how they related to and viewed healthcare administrators, how they interacted with each other and with staff, and what cultural dynamics they stimulated.

That entry-level position was a fertile ground for learning, although she didn't realize it at the time. It prepared her for her subsequent roles, including as a consultant to physician groups.

Our point here is simple: Out of the most unassuming jobs sometimes come rich experiences. If you keep an open mind and embrace these opportunities, instead of taking them for granted, you'll find yourself pleasantly surprised by the career lessons and insights they offer.

No matter what position you hold today and no matter how you feel about it, you must give it the respect it deserves. Make the most of it (more on this later in the chapter), and be grateful for the opportunity. Show up and be stellar at your job every day.

DO MAKE IT HAPPEN

"It" is whatever you want it to be—a promotion, a C-suite or senior management position, a higher salary, a coveted project, and so on. Don't just sit around and wait for the perfect position, the perfect project, or the perfect salary. Keep your eyes open for new or additional opportunities. Volunteer. Identify a need and fill it. Choose a problem and solve it. Define what you want, be prepared to do the work involved, and ask for the opportunity to pursue it. Be specific, and be certain that you have the time to invest.

Making something happen is about taking an initiative, about taking the reins of your own career path. Following are examples of how two professionals made the big leaps happen for themselves early on in their careers.

John's Story

John started his career at the bottom of the corporate ladder. He was so low on the rung, he joked, that he wasn't sure if he was even on the ladder at all! His title sounded nice enough—Junior Analyst—but the job itself was the very definition of entry level. His desk was right next to the copy machine, which was convenient, as copying was among his foremost responsibilities.

Unsatisfied with his job, John began to look around him—literally. He noticed a stack of dusty banker's boxes in the office. They contained old, forgotten collection files. He approached his supervisors and asked if he could sift through the boxes and address the accounts. He got the go-ahead.

Slowly but surely, John dug in and reconciled each account. His work led to the bank recouping money owed; these were dollars that would have remained in boxes had he not volunteered to revisit the accounts. His initiative, his willingness to do the grunt work everyone else avoided, and his strong work ethic that made him go above and beyond his expected duties resulted in his advancement to collector and then loan officer. He spent a decade as a vice president, and today he is a bank president.

Mallory's Story

Mallory is an emerging leader in healthcare. Her story perfectly illustrates how taking the initiative can move you many steps forward on your career path. Here she is in her own words.

"I introduced myself to the CEO after my graduate class took a level 1 trauma tour of his facility. I told him I had grown up in a neighboring county and have always admired the mission of the organization. I told him I knew the excellent work he was doing to change the culture here, and I would love to discuss any opportunity to complete an administrative internship to learn from him and his team. He scheduled a meeting, and we discussed that the organization did not have a formal internship program. After some discussion, he offered me an opportunity to help build a program that summer.

"The internship structure began with biweekly meetings with the CEO and COO so that I could consistently communicate with and learn from them. We built a schedule where I spent a couple of weeks with each VP and their direct reports, holding introductory meetings, taking tours, and attending department meetings. My rotations covered departments such as operations, nursing, medical staff, quality, community health, and IT. I also attended all executive and board meetings. I worked on different projects for the VPs. There was not a closed door, which made for a great learning environment.

"At the end of the summer, we mutually agreed to extend the internship through my second year of MHA studies. My role was redefined to focus on more in-depth projects in finance and IT. I worked on many projects with the CFO. I continued to attend senior-level meetings and board meetings, and I prepared reports for some senior meetings. I continued to serve on the quarterly leadership institute planning committee (and I still do today). I spent some time in planning meetings and steering committees but had no direct responsibility. I continued to work with the CFO on projects and enjoyed his leadership and teaching style immensely.

"During my internship, I was supposed to focus mainly on finance and community health, along with other small responsibilities in various other areas. But community health had new leadership, and I was struggling with gaining traction in projects there. When I told the CFO I had more time to give him, he assigned me to the waiver program, giving me a more visible role in the community and exposing me to new experiences. My life changed overnight. The waiver program has been an incredible career opportunity. It has contributed to my success in my role."

DON'T GET COMFORTABLE

When you get comfortable, you stop trying new approaches and you stop stretching past your comfort zone. And you wait for, not seek, challenges that keep you on your toes, keep your adrenaline pumping, or get your heart racing. But those who achieve greatness rarely wait. Instead, they hunt, fully knowing that any short-term discomfort from such challenges is a small price to pay for long-term success.

So what are these challenges? They could be anything from adopting a bold strategy to setting (and achieving) stretch goals to defying conventions. The idea here is to take a risk and to try new things, even if it means failing, so that you can learn and grow.

Early in her career, Natalie applied for jobs for which she wasn't *fully* qualified (see Chapter 8 for another facet of this story). For example, if the job posting called for seven to ten years' experience and she only had three to five years under her belt, it didn't stop her from applying. Of course, she met all the other qualifications and could back up her application with references, a record of solid work performance, and relevant skills and training. And of course, she disclosed her lack of years of experience. But she took calculated risks to at least be seen and be considered and at best be given a chance to prove herself. She was stretching, reaching to get her foot in the door.

This strategy not only opened doors but also allowed her to skip multiple rungs on the proverbial career ladder. This example may especially resonate with fresh-out-of-school careerists trying to land their first jobs but running straight into a requirement they can't fill yet. It's a problem faced by generation after generation of job seekers: Every hiring organization wants a certain amount of on-the-job experience. But young applicants can't fill that qualification if they are not given the opportunity to gain the experience required.

Don't get lulled by the routine of your job. Teach yourself a new skill while you're at it. While in school, Natalie used to work at a chain clothing store at the mall. She knew she wasn't going to work there forever, so she focused on developing new skills. Not only did she get good at anticipating and meeting the needs of the customers, but she also learned how to input via ten key. When the store wasn't busy, she rang up purchases by typing in SKU numbers into the system rather than scanning the item tags. She timed herself each time and got better and better. Before too long she had mastered the skill and was just as fast manually entering the SKU numbers as scanning them. She still uses the ten key skill today, not to mention the customer service skills she developed.

Whatever you do, get into the habit of challenging and stretching yourself. Don't simply float along. Make some waves.

DO CHART A CAREER PATH

Put pen to paper and write out a path or plan for your career. Make it specific, manage or keep an eye on it, measure your progress against it, and modify it when needed. Most important, stick to it.

Not many things go exactly as planned (Laurie's nonlinear career path is a perfect example of this), but nothing goes anywhere (only round and round in a circle perhaps) without a plan. We can't promise that your career path will lead you to your desired destination, but we can guarantee that, just by charting a path, you're already ahead of the others who don't/won't take the time to sit down and write a plan.

If you need help charting this path or are unclear about what a healthcare career path looks like, consult your mentor or a seasoned administrator or even your own boss. Don't hesitate to interview leaders in your organization or the industry (you can meet them when you attend national events like ACHE's Congress on Healthcare Leadership). Start a conversation: "So, you're a chief strategy officer, what does that entail?" "What projects are you involved in right now?" "How does your job relate to the rest of the organization?" Be a student of your own profession. Then, use that knowledge to chart your own path.

Now here are the *buts*:

1. *But you have to be a doer.* Charting a path—even if it's color coded, laminated, animated, graphic designed, and Instagrammed—is not enough. You have do the hard work. The path is merely a guideline and isn't going to walk itself.

2. *But you have to be realistic.* You can accelerate the timing of your plan goals all you want, but be prepared for disappointment when you don't hit those time frames. Manage your own expectations. Know that you're going to have to apply some elbow grease and pay your dues. The leaders and other healthcare professionals before you poured blood, sweat, and tears into their paths. Expect to do the same. Make room for failures, mistakes, and rejections (see Chapter 8). Setbacks are learning opportunities, but they can unexpectedly derail your path. They will happen, but you can't schedule them.

DO ACT *AS IF*

This goes back to our personal brand discussion in Chapter 5. Carry yourself *as if* you are already in the position you aspire to have. We're talking character-based conduct here, not inflated ego. When you act *as if*, you're likely to make a positive impression and to be regarded as someone who is ready or at least has the potential for the next level. Plus, when you act *as if* and back that up with your strengths (including self-awareness, strong character, and commitment and self-discipline), people will see you as indispensable. You'll be that person everyone thinks they can't do without, that person whom everyone hates to see go at the end of the day. (As Natalie's mom advised her: "Work in such a way that when it's time to go, they hate to see you leave.")

Dress the Part

Top-notch leaders don't just act like top-notch leaders, they look like them, too. Again, dress *as if*. If your role calls for business casual attire, press the envelope and wear the sharpest business attire (if the organizational culture and situation allows, of course). Invest in a power suit—that one tailored piece that makes you feel more confident, taller, and brighter. Polish your shoes. And let your smile be your best accessory. You'll be amazed at how good dressing well makes you feel and how differently others treat you.

Be Authentic

We understand that sometimes when people hear "acting/dressing as if," they immediately think that only those who present themselves in such a way can succeed. Not true, and not what we're saying. Figure out who you are first (again, practice self-reflection). Then, conduct and dress yourself according to the true you. Do polish yourself, because the more put together you look, the more you and what you have to offer shine and the less likely your appearance will serve as a distraction. You don't have to wear designer clothes or trendy pieces (who has the budget for that?!), but you do have to follow the organization's dress code or standard professional clothing.

The more important thing to remember is to be authentic. Don't dress and act/talk exactly like someone else; that person is already taken. You do you—the best version of you. If you don't, you will at some point find yourself miserable and others will think you're a fraud.

With the combination of good attitude and good look, you'll feel different—as if you can go anywhere and accomplish anything. You can transform a job you feel is not the right fit for you into one that is a beneficial learning opportunity. The job itself remains the same. It's your mind-set that changes.

DO STAND OUT

You may not want to be in your current position for the rest of your life, but are you actively doing something about it? For many, the path to the next level often seems littered with obstacles and delays. You yearn to run but feel fenced in. You're revving your engine, but the light hasn't turned green. We know; we've been there.

One of the surest ways to get a chance, a break, or a "yes" is to be a contributor. Organizations—healthcare facilities included—are filled with people who don't want to step up. They are filled with critics and cynics and standbys. So people like you—with skills and talents and ambition—are certainly wanted and needed. Take the initiative (see John's and Mallory's stories earlier in the chapter) and stand up and stand out.

Know your strengths. What can you do that no one else can? What can you do better and faster and longer than anyone else can? Is there a need that's not obvious but has to be filled anyway? Can you create a need for what you can do? For example, you could volunteer to take the minutes for a senior management meeting (a meeting you might otherwise not be invited to). If you don't show up one day, people will start looking for you. Just by showing up all the time and being the person who does something, you've planted a seed that you're *supposed* to be there, that you belong. And people may need you for other projects—big and small.

DO MAKE THE BOSS LOOK GOOD

It may be tough to overcome the stigma attached to the notion of "making the boss look good." After all, nobody wants to be labeled a suck-up. It's certainly a delicate situation. On one hand, you want to endear yourself to the boss. On the other hand, you don't want to be alienated from the rest of the team.

Think of it this way: You need to look out for what is best for you and your career. If that means making the boss look good by doing a great job, so be it. Plenty of your peers want the role and responsibilities you'll possibly land by taking the initiative to work closely with the boss, but they're either too afraid to pursue the opportunity or they don't want to put in the extra work. If they ostracize you because of that, then that's on them, not you.

Now, let's be very clear on one thing: We aren't giving you permission to be a suck-up! We're simply encouraging you to be a key contributor, to be that go-to person, to pay your dues.

An organization client of Laurie uses a term for people who don't want to get involved when they see a problem: "Short arm syndrome." It describes those who pull their arms back, palms facing outward, and say, "Hey, that's not my job!" The opposite of short-arm syndrome is represented by those who are ready and willing to help, take responsibility, and be the go-to person. A little dirt under your fingernails, so to speak, is a badge of honor! Go for it. Extend those arms to the boss.

Why Do It?

  I. *It demonstrates your promotion worthiness or potential.*
     Let's face it, managers initiate most career advances for

their staff. Knocking the supervisor's socks off just may mean a little more cash in your pocket, a nice reference or recommendation or write-up in your employee file, or even a promotion offer. You may not be a senior team member now, but if you consistently prove yourself to be an ace, your boss may just start to visualize you as an individual worthy of promotion.

2. *It instills humility in you.* By looking out for another person, it solidifies that you're a member of the team, which is something bigger than yourself.

3. *It gives you valuable in-the-trenches experience.* Often, focusing on your boss and making her look good takes you outside of your day-to-day responsibilities. So not only do you earn brownie points with the boss, but you also garner new experiences you would not have had at your desk.

How Should I Do It?

1. *Go above and beyond.* It's not enough to do (and do well) what's expected of you. You have to also volunteer to do tasks that are not in your job description, that just came up, or that no one else wants to do. And you have to give your best work, not half-baked attempts or bare minimums just to get it over with. Find ways to show you are willing and capable for these extra opportunities. Be so good that you convince everyone you are indispensable.

2. *Share your strengths.* Master organizer and coordinator? IT genius? Superb troubleshooter, writer, negotiator? Charmer? Customer service maven? Finance expert? Whatever your thing, let it be known. This isn't bragging about what you can do. This is informing those who need to know that you're available to help in specific areas when needed.

3. *Offer solutions.* Organizations are fraught with people who like to complain about everything that's wrong. Instead of jumping on that bandwagon, dare to be different by offering workable solutions to those problems. Leverage your skills, talents, and energy to take the initiative and improve your organization, as opposed to adding to the problem or maintaining the status quo.

DO WIN EMPLOYEES OVER, ESPECIALLY THOSE OLDER THAN YOU

Winning people over is a matter of trust. That means you're in it for the long haul, not a quick sprint. It's not easy, but then again, nothing worth having is. In healthcare, it is incredibly common for your employees to be older than you—often, by several decades. After all, four generations of workers serve in healthcare facilities, and many clinical and administrative positions are held by seasoned professionals.

So many challenges come with this younger boss–older employee dynamic. We both have experienced this, and we still do. Laurie, in particular, was responsible for managing more than three dozen employees when she was only 22. Every single one of them was older; one nurse's date of hire was in the same year Laurie was born. She heard comments such as, "I wonder how long 'til blondie gets chewed up and spit out!" and "I've watched so many managers come and go, and when you leave I will still be here."

As an emerging healthcare leader, you have to be prepared for this eventuality. Exhibit 13.1 offers tips for establishing rapport with your employees despite the generation gaps.

Exhibit 13.1 Tips for Managing Employees Older Than You

1. *Treat all employees with genuine respect.* Your character and conduct trump almost all your other accomplishments. If employees see that you sincerely care about their roles and needs, they won't see your age. Your date of birth will be ignored and your qualities as a person and as a leader will shine. As the saying goes, "People don't care how much you know until they know how much you care."

2. *Listen.* Get in the habit of seeking out conversations with all employees, communicating often with members of your teams and departments. The more you get to know your staff through these conversations, the better you'll be able to provide resources. And the more you know each person—their talents, abilities, and contributions—the more effectively you can engage, inspire, and acknowledge them.

3. *Lead by example.* Set the tone by exhibiting the integrity, work ethic, and attitude you hope to see in your team. Twenty-somethings often get a bad reputation for being entitled. If your contributions and conduct are strong, they'll speak for you. Show up early, stay late, and be a team player.

4. *Show humility.* Acknowledge the value of others, and generously give credit where credit is due. Don't be afraid to say, "I don't know the answer, but I will find out." There is no better way than that to prove your humility or to build rapport and trust with your employees—especially those who might have issues with the age gap. As you grow into your career, be humble about the fact that no one—not even you—can know everything all the time. There are too many moving parts in healthcare. But everyone is an expert in their respective areas. The hospital's compliance officer, for example, may know the ins and outs of Joint Commission accreditation better than he knows himself, but he may be at a loss when asked about CLIA waiver certification for the laboratory or what the oncology floor requires for its IV competencies.

5. *Learn from the wise.* You will always have smart people around you from whom you can learn (look at your board of career advisors, for example). These are individuals whose experiences and expertise far outweigh yours. As a leader, your role isn't to be the utmost authority on all matters but to strategically align resources to organizational goals. Glean wisdom from those who have been around longer than you have. If they've been there, done that—especially for a long time within the current organization—don't hesitate to leverage that experience. Kindly, of course. Doing so could equip you with valuable insight. Learn from their mistakes and lessons learned.

Remember These

- Out of the most unassuming jobs sometimes come rich experiences. If you keep an open mind and embrace these opportunities, instead of taking them for granted, you'll find yourself pleasantly surprised by the career lessons and insights they offer.

- Keep your eyes open for new or additional opportunities. Volunteer. Identify a need and fill it. Choose a problem and solve it. Define what you want, be prepared to do the work involved, and ask for the opportunity to pursue it.

- Don't get lulled by the routine of your job. Teach yourself a new skill while you're at it.

- Make your boss look good by being his or her go-to person or key contributor. Knocking the supervisor's socks off just may mean a little more cash in your pocket, a nice reference or recommendation or write-up in your employee file, or even a promotion offer.

- In healthcare, it is incredibly common for your employees to be older than you—often, by several decades. Your character and conduct trump almost all your other accomplishments. If employees see that you sincerely care about their roles and needs, they won't care about the generation gap.

Books That Teach, Advise, and Inspire Us

Laurie's List

1. *The Advantage: Why Organizational Health Trumps Everything Else in Business* by Patrick Lencioni

2. *Strengths Based Leadership: Great Leaders, Teams, and Why People Follow* by Tom Rath and Barrie Conchie

3. *The Speed of Trust: The One Thing That Changes Everything* by Stephen M. R. Covey

4. *Drive: The Surprising Truth About What Motivates Us* by Daniel H. Pink

5. *Leaders Eat Last: Why Some Teams Pull Together and Others Don't* by Simon Sinek

6. *Wooden on Leadership: How to Create a Winning Organization* by John Wooden and Steve Jamison

7. *Daring Greatly: How the Courage to Be Vulnerable Transforms the Way We Live, Love, Parent, and Lead* by Brene Brown

8. *Rework* by Jason Fried and David Heinemeier Hansson

9. *Outliers: The Story of Success* by Malcolm Gladwell

10. *Linchpin: Are You Indispensable?* by Seth Godin

11. *Failing Forward: Turning Mistakes into Stepping Stones for Success* by John Maxwell

(continued)

12. *Executive Excellence: Protocols for Healthcare Leaders*, 2nd ed., by Carson Dye

13. *The Last Lecture* by Randy Pausch

Natalie's List

1. *How to Win Friends and Influence People* by Dale Carnegie

2. *Management Lessons from Mayo Clinic: Inside One of the World's Most Admired Service Organizations* by Leonard L. Berry and Kent D. Seltman

3. *Over Our Heads: An Analogy on Healthcare, Good Intentions, and Unforeseen Consequences* by Rulon Stacey

4. *The One Minute Manager* by Kenneth H. Blanchard and Spencer Johnson

5. *Developing the Leader Within You* by John C. Maxwell

6. *HBR's 10 Must Reads: On Leadership, On Managing People, On Managing Yourself* (compilation of articles)

7. *Executive Charisma: Six Steps to Mastering the Art of Leadership* by D. A. Benton

8. *Good to Great: Why Some Companies Make the Leap . . . And Others Don't* by Jim Collins

9. *The Effective Executive: The Definitive Guide to Getting the Right Things Done* by Peter F. Drucker

10. *The Practice of Management* by Peter F. Drucker

11. *The Servant: A Simple Story About the True Essence of Leadership* by James C. Hunter

12. *Fierce Conversations: Achieving Success at Work and in Life One Conversation at a Time* by Susan Scott

13. *Execution: The Discipline of Getting Things Done* by Larry Bossidy and Ram Charan

About the Authors

Laurie K. Baedke, MHA, FACHE, FACMPE, is a bank executive with broad experience building companies and leading organizational culture, brand strategy, and business development. In her role as chief brand officer of Core Bank in Omaha, Nebraska, she provides leadership to the organization's brand strategy, culture development, and healthcare banking teams.

Laurie has specific expertise in physician practice management, leadership development, and organizational change. She is an active mentor and advisor to emerging leaders and entrepreneurs, start-up companies, and small businesses; a frequent speaker at national conferences; and a facilitator at association and company retreats. She holds a bachelor's degree in human services and business administration and a master's degree in healthcare administration. She is a Fellow of the American College of Healthcare Executives (ACHE) and the American College of Medical Practice Executives, as well as a member of the Medical Group Management Association. In addition, she is one of only five independent consultants globally to hold certification by The Gallup Organization as a strengths performance coach.

A recipient of numerous awards—including the Nebraska ACHE Regent's Early Career Excellence Award and the Region 5 ACHE Regent's Award for Healthcare Excellence—Laurie considers her contributions to her profession and the community as a very important part of her life. She is a member of the adjunct faculty at Creighton University, Methodist College, Bellevue University, and

Clarkson College. She has served as a mentor in Gallup's Entrepreneur Accelerator System, is a graduate of the Omaha Chamber of Commerce Leadership Omaha Class 35, and sits on the advisory board for several start-up companies. Additionally, she is a board member of the ACHE Regent's Advisory Council and the Heartland Healthcare Executive Group, and she has served on ACHE's Chapter Committee; Early Careerist Committee; and Products, Programming, and Services Committee.

Natalie D. Lamberton, MBA/MHA, FACHE, is the CEO of Regency Hospital of Fort Worth. Her career in healthcare leadership has been extensive. Previously, she served as the director of neurosciences at the Medical Center of Aurora; as an administrator in Presbyterian Health System, where she oversaw a $190 million construction project for a new hospital; as CEO of the Haxtun Hospital District, which comprised a hospital, an extended care unit, and three primary care clinics servicing communities within a 300-square-mile radius; and as the director of retail services of the Poudre Valley Health System, where she designed, developed, and implemented the corporate strategic plan for the division. In addition, she was the first postgraduate administrative fellow for the Poudre Valley Health System.

Natalie is the recipient of the 2014 American College of Healthcare Executives (ACHE) Exemplary Service Award, 2013 ACHE Distinguished Service Award, 2011 ACHE Service Award, and the 2009 ACHE Regent's Early Careerist Award, among others. Currently, she is on the ache.org editorial board, and she has served as a board member of the ACHE Regent's Advisory Council and on Health Administration Press's Management Series editorial board. She also served on the Colorado Association of Healthcare Executives board for several years and on various councils and committees of the Colorado Hospital Association. She is a Fellow of ACHE and is a member of the National Association of Health Services Executives. In addition, she has been a guest lecturer (discussing leadership and management) for Creighton University's

Heider College of Business MBA program, the University of Iowa's College of Public Health MHA–MBA program, the University of New Mexico Anderson Executive MBA program, Brigham Young University's Marriott School MPA program, and the University of Texas at Dallas Naveen Jindal School of Management graduate program. Her passion is mentoring and inspiring new leaders.

She earned a BS degree in molecular biology and US history from the University of New Mexico, graduating cum laude. While there, she ran track and field on a full-ride Division I scholarship. A recipient of the distinguished University of Colorado Hoffman–Binger Graduate Presidential Scholarship, Natalie holds a dual MBA and MHA degree. A former teacher, she taught science and history at the middle school and high school levels; she also was a freshman biology instructor at the Community College of Denver.